Praise for *Am I Cut Out for This?*

"Being an educational leader is just about impossible—full of crazy expectations, tough calls, and constant intensity. *Am I Cut Out for This?* doesn't just acknowledge these realities, it tackles them head-on with humor, insight, and real-world strategies. Elizabeth Dampf delivers a refreshingly readable guide, blending compelling storytelling with practical advice."

—**Simon Rodberg,** author, *What If I'm Wrong? And Other Key Questions for Decisive School Leadership;* executive director, Lee Montessori Public Charter School, Washington, DC

"Elizabeth Dampf delivers an essential guide for every school leader who has ever wrestled with self-doubt. *Am I Cut Out for This?* is a powerful, heartfelt, and practical road map that transforms uncertainty into confidence, isolation into community, and hesitation into action. With authenticity and wisdom, Dampf equips leaders with the mindset, strategies, and support they need to navigate the challenges of leadership with purpose and resilience. This book isn't just a read, it's a companion for the journey, offering encouragement that will stay with you long after you turn the last page."

—**Sean Gaillard,** principal; author, *The Pepper Effect*; podcaster, *Principal Liner Notes*

AM I CUT OUT FOR THIS?

ELIZABETH DAMPF

AM I CUT OUT FOR THIS?

AN EDUCATIONAL LEADER'S GUIDE TO NAVIGATING SELF-DOUBT

Arlington, Virginia USA

2111 Wilson Boulevard, Suite 300 • Arlington, VA 22201 USA
Phone: 800-933-2723 or 703-578-9600
Website: www.ascd.org • Email: member@ascd.org
Author guidelines: www.ascd.org/write

Richard Culatta, *Chief Executive Officer;* Anthony Rebora, *Chief Content Officer;* Genny Ostertag, *Managing Director, Book Acquisitions & Editing;* Susan Hills, *Senior Acquisitions Editor;* Mary Beth Nielsen, *Director, Book Editing;* Jennifer L. Morgan, *Editor;* Georgia Park, *Graphic Designer;* Valerie Younkin, *Senior Production Designer;* Circle Graphics, *Typesetter;* Kelly Marshall, *Production Manager;* Shajuan Martin, *E-Publishing Specialist;* Christopher Logan, *Senior Production Specialist*

Copyright © 2025 ASCD. All rights reserved. It is illegal to reproduce copies of this work in print or electronic format (including reproductions displayed on a secure intranet or stored in a retrieval system or other electronic storage device from which copies can be made or displayed) without the prior written permission of the publisher. By purchasing only authorized electronic or print editions and not participating in or encouraging piracy of copyrighted materials, you support the rights of authors and publishers. Readers who wish to reproduce or republish excerpts of this work in print or electronic format may do so for a small fee by contacting the Copyright Clearance Center (CCC), 222 Rosewood Dr., Danvers, MA 01923, USA (phone: 978-750-8400; fax: 978-646-8600; web: www.copyright.com). To inquire about site licensing options or any other reuse, contact ASCD Permissions at www.ascd.org/permissions or permissions@ascd.org. For a list of vendors authorized to license ASCD ebooks to institutions, see www.ascd.org/epubs. Send translation inquiries to translations@ascd.org.

ASCD® is a registered trademark of Association for Supervision and Curriculum Development. All other trademarks contained in this book are the property of, and reserved by, their respective owners, and are used for editorial and informational purposes only. No such use should be construed to imply sponsorship or endorsement of the book by the respective owners.

All web links in this book are correct as of the publication date below but may have become inactive or otherwise modified since that time. If you notice a deactivated or changed link, please email books@ascd.org with the words "Link Update" in the subject line. In your message, please specify the web link, the book title, and the page number on which the link appears.

PAPERBACK ISBN: 978-1-4166-3368-6   ASCD product #125007   n6/25
PDF EBOOK ISBN: 978-1-4166-3369-3; see Books in Print for other formats.
Quantity discounts are available: email programteam@ascd.org or call 800-933-2723, ext. 5773, or 703-575-5773. For desk copies, go to www.ascd.org/deskcopy.

Library of Congress Cataloging-in-Publication Data

Names: Dampf, Elizabeth, 1985- author
Title: Am I cut out for this? : an educational leader's guide to navigating self-doubt / Elizabeth Dampf.
Description: Arlington, Virginia : ASCD, [2025] | Includes bibliographical references and index.
Identifiers: LCCN 2025004840 (print) | LCCN 2025004841 (ebook) | ISBN 9781416633686 paperback | ISBN 9781416633693 pdf | ISBN 9781416633709 epub
Subjects: LCSH: Educational leadership—Psychological aspects—United States | Self-doubt—United States | School management and organization—United States
Classification: LCC LB2806 .D237 2025 (print) | LCC LB2806 (ebook) | DDC 371.2/011—dc23/eng/20250421
LC record available at https://lccn.loc.gov/2025004840
LC ebook record available at https://lccn.loc.gov/2025004841

---

34 33 32 31 30 29 28 27 26 25   1 2 3 4 5 6 7 8 9 10 11 12

AM I CUT OUT FOR THIS?

Introduction: Doubt Comes Naturally;
  Confidence Takes Work 1

1. The Jittery Innovator 9

2. The Empty Empathizer 28

3. The Punching Bag 44

4. The Struggling Salesperson 64

5. The Mob Mollifier 86

6. The Short Straw 106

7. The Instructional Impostor 124

Conclusion 139

References 142

Index 143

About the Author 147

Introduction:
Doubt Comes Naturally;
Confidence Takes Work

It's not that grad school was useless, exactly. It's just that I have a few notes. Sure, learning about leadership theory was cool, but the syllabus seemed to be missing a few things. Where was the seminar on handling an angry mob? On working with your bullying boss? On promoting someone else's unpopular plan?

For every obscure law you studied in your leadership program, there's an essential practice you didn't. Many instructors regard the skills administrators need every day—political acumen, emotional resilience, quick thinking—as innate qualities rather than learnable techniques. The message is clear: *You have it or you don't.* As a newly forged administrator, you find yourself gripping your diploma between white knuckles, hoping you have "it" as you walk into your first leadership position.

On the job, however, everyone sees that diploma as a certificate of omniscience—proof that you were spawned, sterling and immaculate, from an industrial fortress. With an admin degree, you should be able to handle anything thrown at you, right? You should be both supremely knowledgeable and impervious to attack. These expectations only amplify your fears. You did all the reading and attended all the lectures, but none of them prepared you for the bizarre, terrifying, combative world of school administration. *What if I don't have "it"?* you think in panic. *What if I'm a total fraud, a poser who sneaked in while no one was looking? Sooner or later, everyone will realize that I don't belong here.*

And if you think experience will allay these fears, think again. I've been an administrator for over a decade, and I still feel like a rube blundering from one mistake to the next sometimes. In fact, the longer I work in education, the gnarlier those doubts grow. Perhaps you feel this way too. Perhaps the more you learn about leadership, the more you become aware of what you don't know. Why, you wonder, are even veteran leaders hounded with doubts, anxieties, and fears?

I'll tell you why. You work in a system where you must be compliant with edicts from above but also innovative in your thinking; popular with staff but also a hammer when necessary; a political mastermind but also vulnerable and genuine. You must take responsibility for factors beyond your control. If we're being honest, you sometimes end up taking abuse. And you can be fired for failing to meet any of these expectations. Tenure and unions can protect teachers' positions; you, on the other hand, are on a one-year contract that can be terminated the moment your political capital plummets. Throw in factors like lack of readiness and general human error, and it's no wonder you grapple with doubt. Your doubts are not only understandable but wholly justified by the nature of your profession.

Considering its prevalence, you'd think every school leader would be talking about self-doubt. It could be the hottest topic in meetings, the theme of entire conferences, the pinnacle of leader training—but it's not. On the contrary, self-doubt is a taboo subject, a perceived weakness, and a shameful secret. Leaders discover this harsh reality on their first day in office. Voice doubt in your own ability, and your colleagues—even your supervisor—will likely respond by telling you to suck it up or fake it till you make it. Compassionate colleagues might blithely tell you to trust yourself, as though it were that easy. All of this feedback reinforces the idea that you must bury your fears, misgivings, and uncertainty in a secret lair, never to be acknowledged, let alone confronted.

Those bold enough to discuss self-doubt often use the term "impostor syndrome," which evokes chronic illness and suggests sufferers must manage their condition with careful lifestyle choices. Searing self-doubt, however, isn't a "syndrome" to which certain people are especially susceptible. It's a byproduct of the American education system, which exerts ever more pressure on leaders to be experts in everything, instantly capable of handling whatever core-shaking, soul-crushing, high-stakes crisis arises on any given Tuesday. Everyone experiences uncertainty in these circumstances, even if they don't label it with buzzwordy nicknames.

Someone once asked me what affirmation I use when experiencing doubt. Honestly, I found the question infuriating. I know some swear by affirmations and mindfulness, but these practices alone aren't enough. No affirmation could possibly combat the ceaseless, inevitable doubts I have faced as a leader. What single mantra could ever assuage my fear of being caught in a political quagmire, publicly humiliated, and fired for appearances' sake? What mindfulness activity could mitigate my anxiety about being rejected by the very people for whom I've sacrificed my health, peace, and family time? Chant "I am capable and prepared" all you want; it doesn't change the fact that you will regularly face people and situations for which you are, in actuality, unprepared. The hard truth is that, at some point, we will fall short of other people's expectations or fail to rise to certain leadership challenges. For leaders, self-doubt isn't a symptom of an overactive imagination, it's an awareness of what's at stake.

Given this reality, it's time to admit that as a profession, we take entirely the wrong attitude toward self-doubt. We act like self-doubt is an illness to be treated or a character flaw to be corrected. We tie ourselves in knots trying to banish all qualms through palliative self-care. Rather ironically, we compound our sense of inadequacy by feeling guilty about feeling doubtful. (*Why can't I be more confident? I'm so stupid!*) If any of this strikes a chord with you, know this:

1. **You are not alone.** Everyone faces doubt. If they didn't, terms like "impostor syndrome" and techniques like "daily affirmations" wouldn't be so ubiquitous. The sheer demand for self-help advice for leaders implies an epidemic of doubt, even if it's borderline impossible to get them to admit their anxiety to others or even to themselves. It usually takes a crisis to surface a leader's fear that they aren't enough, that they don't have it, that they will one day be exposed as a phony. If you've ever reached out for help after screwing up royally, you probably found yourself flooded with empathy from other leaders who told you in hushed tones that, like you, they often feel like they are walking a tightrope in the dark, one misstep away from disaster. In those somber moments, you realized you're not the only one wondering if you're cut out for this whole leadership gig. It's a testament both to the universality of doubt and to the shame associated with it that only a crisis can bring certain truths to the fore.

2. **You are not incompetent.** I'm not placating you with a glib affirmation, nor am I suggesting you won't struggle, fail, and question your abilities like the rest of us. Look at it logically, though. What kind of person would you be if you bullheadedly forged ahead with no doubts, no hesitations, no reflections? Have you ever met a good leader who staunchly insisted on following only their way, never questioning their beliefs and fully convinced of their own omniscience? *Please.* Far from capable, leaders like that are shortsighted, delusional, and, yes, incompetent. On the other hand, leaders who lean into their own vulnerability, their own potential for error, and the possibility that they may not have what it takes in every situation are the ones who grow the fastest. They also avoid disaster more easily than the blowhards because they reflect more deeply and collaborate more readily. Thus, the mere fact that you are interrogating your fitness to lead suggests that you are a reflective practitioner, eager to grow to your full potential. Incompetent people don't do that.
3. **Your doubts do not hinder your leadership ability.** This is easier said than believed because of our cultural mythology treating leadership as an innate talent rather than a learnable skill. True, some people are more inclined toward leadership, just as some are more inclined toward playing music or practicing medicine, but at the end of the day, leader, musician, and physician are all skill-based professions. If they weren't, you could never improve; you'd be stuck at whatever level of talent you were born with. Subscribing to the "you have it or you don't" mentality gives our doubts an extra weapon: the blood-chilling suggestion that we *don't* have it, that we're inherently deficient and

always will be. Even the most troubling self-doubts, however, do not erode the concrete skills you've developed over your leadership career. You keep your gains.

All this is to say that doubt is a natural feeling, not an illness to be treated. Still, experiencing doubt can be disturbing, even and especially to veteran administrators. In my long career, my doubts have not abated—if anything, they've increased as I see what's at stake for myself and my students and recognize, with ever greater clarity, my own inadequacy. I can't always respond perfectly, I can't always have the impact I want, and I'm usually one political crisis away from a nervous breakdown. It reminds me of C. S. Lewis's words: "No man knows how bad he is till he has tried very hard to be good" (Lewis, 1952, p. 142). As our skills grow, so does our awareness of our own shortcomings. Cold comfort, I know.

So if we can't—and maybe shouldn't—banish, treat, or ignore the doubts that plague us, how should we respond to them? The first step is to understand what triggers our doubts. Self-doubt is often situational. We don't spend every second of every day feeling like failures, but certain challenges send us spiraling. Analyzing those instigating situations can help illuminate why and how the doubt creeps in, which is essential to reframing our attitude toward it. We can see that doubt is not the inevitable result of our own deficiency but rather the consequence of working in a tense, high-stakes environment that demands more of every educator than they can possibly give.

When we understand the sources of our misgivings, we can plan skillful, confident responses. This is the best approach to self-doubt. We're not trying to cure ourselves with a regimen of affirmations and magical thinking; we're looking reality in the face and making logical, capable, effective plans. We're not fixing our heads but refining our skills, especially those required in the situations that trigger us the most. We're anticipating the presence of doubt and devising a context-based response.

To that end, I present seven scenarios featuring roles administrators play that can make us question whether we belong in educational leadership: the jittery innovator, the empty empathizer, the punching bag, the struggling salesperson, the mob mollifier, the short straw, and the instructional impostor. Like me, you probably find yourself playing these roles every year but still feel uncertain as you walk into the spotlight. The solutions I propose aren't stale mantras or cuddly self-help techniques. Instead, I identify the aspects of each situation that ignite doubts and suggest ways to respond with confidence. The goal is to first think through why and how doubts grip us, then strategize our counterattack.

Full disclosure: This book isn't a compendium of academic research. It's a practical field guide based on my experience. I wrote it because I'm weary of being told how to handle the pressure of my job by people who have never actually done my job. If you, too, would like to enter a discussion around educational leadership that is firmly grounded in the specific, sometimes brutal, reality of the profession, you bought the right book. I won't blow smoke with shallow inspiration or dispense dime store advice for curing what ails you. I also won't tell you whether you should stay in leadership. I will, however, empathize deeply with your plight. Like you, I sometimes doubt my ability to survive—let alone succeed—in a career that demands more of me than I think I can give. So let's face the facts together.

Hopefully, this book helps you feel seen. It's hard to feel genuine connections in a professionally inhibited field where administrators keep their doubts to themselves, but maybe reading this book will help you feel less isolated. It should also help you feel less guilty about your doubt, knowing that it's not a disease. Finally, it should prepare you to encounter doubt-inducing situations with the aim of performing well, even if you don't feel confident at first. I hope that, as you refine your skills and work your way through ever more perilous scenarios, you find the stigma around self-doubt giving way to empathy for yourself and your fellow leaders.

1

The Jittery Innovator

Priya gets positively high on the heady fumes of innovation. Always a visionary, she dreams of radically transforming teaching and learning at her school. It's why she applied for the principal position. She visits the sometimes sleepy classrooms in her building and sees what they could be: vibrant, cutting-edge ecosystems that produce dynamic minds and engaged citizens. Her dream of helping her school reach its full potential inspires her every waking hour, in school and out, and she believes with all her heart that her plans could spark a renaissance.

Or at least, she believed it until she got the job. Now that she's behind the big desk, guilt, fear, and self-consciousness have squashed her hopeful beliefs. Priya's innovative ideas still inspire *her*, but they don't inspire her staff. On the contrary, teachers counter any new proposal with everything from skepticism to outright hostility. Two months into the school year, and the only "radical transformation" Priya has seen is in her morale.

Priya is the fourth principal the school has had in 10 years. Each successive leader has marched in with grand plans to raise abysmal test scores and improve school culture and marched out having done neither. Teachers don't expect Priya to last any longer than her predecessors; they will be there, doing their own thing, long after she and her schemes have moved along.

Priya knows her ambitious blueprint for school improvement is what secured her the principal job. The hiring committee was very clear: They wanted a "turnaround principal" who could produce serious improvement within the first two years. It felt like an opportunity tailor-made for Priya, who has always envisioned herself as a zealous innovator and couldn't wait to lead the charge. She's done everything she learned in graduate school: articulated a research-based improvement plan, communicated SMART goals to staff, and established a system of professional learning and support. She's built relationships with teachers and tried to leverage those relationships to inspire change. She's partnered with community organizations, professional consultants, and more.

But every day is a battle. The apathy is what gets her: No matter how energized she is about her ideas, the staff seem implacable. Hours of well-designed professional learning have had no impact whatsoever on her teachers' practice. True, they comply with the minimum expectations stated in the improvement plan, but halfhearted implementation removes any chance the strategies will work. Priya doesn't want to resort to threats, disciplinary measures, or coercive methods to enact change, but her positive advertising campaign isn't working. In fact, the resistance from staff is starting to make her doubt whether her plans would work even if implemented perfectly. Maybe they are terrible plans. Maybe she's a terrible leader. All that research, all those ideas, and for what? A never-ending fight? Priya wonders if she will spend the rest of her career devising plans, battling resistance, succumbing to inertia, and moving to a new school every few years to start the cycle again.

Debrief the Doubts

We all want to be change leaders—in fact, the ability to successfully deliver change is probably the most coveted skill in school administration. Ever since the No Child Left Behind (NCLB) Act ushered in a focus on U.S. school reform in 2002, leaders have raced to demonstrate their innovative prowess. Graduate programs focused extensively—sometimes exclusively—on change theory. Districts competed for grant money by proposing elaborate reorganizations. Charter schools sprang up, offering inventive new solutions to age-old problems. The concept of a "turnaround principal" spread like wildfire.

The 2015 repeal of NCLB did little to diminish the nationwide preoccupation with educational reform. To this day, most districts prioritize school improvement plans, student growth metrics, and other NCLB holdovers either to meet state requirements or because they find value in these measures. Like it or not, we will all roll out sweeping changes in our districts at some point.

Such rollouts can shake you to your core. No matter how passionately you believe in the reforms you're enacting, your actions and decisions will be under attack from the moment you share your plans with your school. The first assailant is, predictably and understandably, staff resistance—teachers have weathered constant change for decades, often without having a voice in decisions that affect them, and their indignation and exhaustion are justified. Moreover, like those at Priya's school, teachers usually outlast their principals. The average principal stays at a school for only four years, a brevity of tenure that affects both staff morale and student performance (Levin & Bradley, 2019). And that statistic may worsen: 40 percent of principals expect to leave the profession as a result of post-pandemic burnout

(National Association of Secondary School Principals, 2021). Bluntly, teachers aren't wrong to assume that their leaders won't stick around or to question the changes demanded by someone who is quite possibly just passing through. "How do you know this will improve student learning, behavior, or well-being?" is a perfectly reasonable question for teachers to ask, yet all too often, it surprises or even angers leaders. To be fair to leaders, the skepticism and questioning aren't always conveyed in a reasonable manner; we've all witnessed the raging tempers and heated words that often accompany change rollouts.

However reasonable, staff resistance can trigger the second assailant: your own jagged, icy doubt. As teachers poke holes in your plan, you question whether it was any good to begin with. You *thought* you'd done enough research and considered the plan from every angle, but now you're not sure. On top of that, you're doubting your own ability to advocate for change. Do you *really* have the stamina to keep up the positive energy in the face of hostile resistance . . and what will that do to your relationships? Are you *absolutely sure* your plans will work . . . and what if they don't? What are you willing to do to make the changes happen . . . and are you prepared to discipline or dismiss noncompliant teachers?

To cap it all off, you must promote your change plan effectively—always a risky undertaking. The right sales pitch can get some teachers to buy in, but the wrong pitch will turn off the whole group. At the end of the day, you have to show the right amount of confidence in your plan and in your staff. Teachers are smart. They've seen administrators come and go on the waves of their grandiose plans. Unfortunately, it's easy to take a wrong turn by accident. While trying to appear confident, you might come across as delusionally cocksure and oblivious to teachers' needs. While selling the merits of the plan, you might look like a smarmy huckster, peddling snake oil to glorify yourself. Even trying to be candid, vulnerable, and open could come across as uncertainty, which is just as damaging as projecting overconfidence. So how do you confidently sell your change plans without overpromising?

Avoid the Pitfalls
Don't Create a Plan in Isolation

We all studied leadership theory. We know, officially, that we shouldn't hatch a plan behind closed doors, but instead should collaborate at every turn. Still, even veteran administrators find themselves caught up in their own grand schemes. You're washing the dishes one night and, suddenly, lightning strikes: *What a brilliant idea! We should do that!* Your naturally innovative tendency kicks in, and you flesh your idea out into an actual plan, maybe bringing in one or two other administrators. Only when it's fully articulated do you involve other staff, usually in the form of "running it past" teacher leaders, union representatives, and others.

Following this path delivers a twofold insult to teachers. Not only does it leave them out of the planning process, by the time they see the plan itself, they get the (usually accurate) impression that the decision to act has already been made and that they are only being "consulted" as a perfunctory display of collaboration. That's the cause of their umbrage. Teachers aren't naturally resistant, but they dislike being left out of decisions that affect them—and who wouldn't?

The most frustrating aspect of this is that teachers are not a monolithic group. Their perspectives are wide-ranging and their needs complex, meaning that you could tie yourself in knots trying to make a decision that pleases everyone. You could work with a diverse committee of teachers, collaboratively create a plan, and some people will *still* hate it. The goal here isn't to generate universal admiration for and immediate buy-in to your plan, it's to avoid the deadliest pitfall of total and utter defiance. The minute you try to roll out a plan you created in isolation, you've lost the battle, if not the war. Bringing in teacher voices demonstrates your willingness to collaborate—and helps keep your plan alive through any initial objections.

Don't Promise Unconditional Success

Yes, you researched. Yes, you found case studies of your ideas working in other schools. But you can't see into the future—and guaranteeing a specific outcome will make you look ridiculous if your plans don't pan out. It will also put you in jeopardy; an unfulfilled promise of success could cost you quite a lot, from the trust of your teachers to the security of your job.

Your motives are pure—you want to inspire confidence in your staff to give them the best chance of success. You want them to see your vision, implement the plan with fidelity, and feel as energized as you do. These are worthy goals; don't sabotage them by using counterproductive tactics like marching in and rallying the troops with galvanizing promises of glory. Teachers have seen that act for years, and to them, it's about as inspirational as a late-night infomercial.

Don't Let Unworthy Questions Derail You

How I wish that all questions were sincere, motivated by curiosity and a desire to do the right thing. Alas, they're not. Unworthy questions lurk behind many of the hands that shoot into the air the moment you introduce a change. If you've ever stood in front of a crowd trying to explain a decision, sell a plan, or uphold unpopular rules, you know exactly what I mean. Questions in the following categories are simply unworthy of educated professionals:

- **Manipulative questions** seek to trap you into an unfavorable position. The speaker wants you to appear foolish, callous, egotistical, or untrustworthy, so they phrase a question with a false premise or dare you to say something that will expose a weakness.
    — "When did the school stop caring about student accountability?"
    — "Is this new grading system going to last longer than the old one?"
- **Disingenuous questions** masquerade as innocent curiosity. The speaker is baiting you into admitting faults or flaws in your plan, hoping to get you to bargain, overexplain, or backpedal.
    — "If the school is taking the locks off our classroom doors, are they giving us bulletproof vests instead?"
    — "This is so much work that we'll have to give up our lunch period to do it. Whom should we send our overtime forms to?"
- **Unrealistic questions** invite you and other listeners to indulge in extremely contrived hypotheticals, rather than sticking to the facts. The speaker wants to make your argument appear absurd by positing an extreme worst-case scenario or disingenuously oversimplifying the situation to suit their purpose.
    — "What happens when the entire math faculty quits because this curriculum is impossible to teach?"

— "What protections will the district provide for teachers who are sued because of this program?"

Unworthy questions are especially infuriating because they come from people you care about. You work hard to build relationships and generate trust only to have someone on your team ask a manipulative, disingenuous question in the middle of a meeting. You feel betrayed. On top of all that, because you want to be the type of open, collaborative leader who embraces dialogue, your first instinct is to answer every question, no matter how unworthy. Dignifying an unworthy question with a serious answer, however, is usually a recipe for disaster.

You can't stop unworthy questions from arising, but you can relegate them to their proper place: the peanut gallery. Don't respond to every unworthy question with a long, serious answer. A short, direct statement is fine, even if it's a deflection: "Thanks for the question. I'd like to discuss that with you later." Even more important, don't let these preposterous questions sabotage your meetings; have the questioners post them in a digital or paper "parking lot" or schedule follow-up meetings if you have to, but keep to your agenda.

Navigate a Path

Sell the Collaboration as Much as the Plan

You've avoided the pitfall of creating a plan in isolation—well done. Now you need to advertise the teamwork far and wide. Every meeting, every conversation you have regarding your new initiative should repeatedly refer to the collaborative process that brought it about, highlighting how representatives from every stakeholder group pooled their talents to create a plan on which they all agreed.

You want to sell the collaboration just as much as you sell the plan itself. When you talk about the initiative in front of staff, try to spend at least half of your total talk time describing how a diverse team banded together to fix a pressing problem. Recall the best moments from the collaborative meetings and explain how thoroughly the group explored all options. Commend the teacher representatives for their conscientious, devoted labor. Tell everyone how lucky you are to work with such innovative educators, who rolled up their sleeves to solve their school's problems with creativity and compassion. Give credit to the teachers for researching options, vetting plans, and picking the right path for the school. Best of all, enlist their help in the advertising campaign; encourage teachers who served on the committee to represent the plan and sell it to their colleagues.

Let me say for the record that I know this advice will only get you so far. I understand perfectly well that teachers sometimes devour colleagues who advocate for change, especially when those colleagues advocate in concert with administrators. I've seen it again and again, and I grow more jaded every time. I have been that teacher advocating change, trying to sell a school improvement plan to furious colleagues because my principal thought the initial rollout would sound better coming from a teacher. When he left the room, I was the one stuck with an angry mob accusing me of wanting them to break their contracts and asking me trick questions they knew I couldn't possibly answer. People I had known for years acted downright viciously toward me, trying to deflate my spirit, and it worked. I never volunteered for another committee again.

I've also seen the situation from the other side. I've watched teachers explain a new curriculum *that they had created* to their peers, who staunchly refused to implement it and shunned the creators. Eventually, we couldn't get any teachers to join improvement committees because they feared social repercussions. It's devastating to see excellent teachers hide their ideas and beg their leaders not to hold them up as an example. It's a natural consequence of incessant change initiatives that go nowhere, but it's still terrible.

All this is to say that even though you and I know that neither collaborating nor promoting the collaboration will guarantee a receptive response, let alone faithful implementation, you're still better off doing it than not for the sake of a few substantial benefits.

First, you will walk away from the process with a team of capable teacher leaders—as long as you arm them with the leadership skills they will need to withstand any resistance they encounter as they promote the initiative. This is where my principal failed me all those years ago: I walked into our rollout meeting with no clue what to expect or how to handle it. Don't let that happen to your teachers. Rather than toss them into a high-stakes situation with no prior experience, scaffold situations in which you enlist their leadership. Support them in explaining the initiative first to a small team, then to a department, then to the whole school. Spend serious time preparing them to defuse tense situations, sharing every strategy you know, including coaching them to answer tricky questions and calibrating their responses with those of the other team members. Listen, empathize, and coach them through the turmoil that will arise when their peers push back. Develop them as leaders one by one, and they will help you shoulder the challenge of enacting change despite resistance.

The other major benefit you gain from selling the collaboration is the protection that comes from being part of a team. A team distributes responsibility, preventing you from being the lone scapegoat for every minute problem that arises. Frankly, it also provides a good default response to complaints. When staff attack the initiative, voicing grievances and attempting to wheedle you into scaling back expectations, you can always say, "I think that's a great topic to discuss with our leadership committee—I'll put it on our next agenda and get back to you." Of course, you need to offer more than lip service; you do, in fact, have to relay concerns to the committee and follow up with teachers, but you gain substantial protection from sharing responsibility for change management with a team.

Selling the collaboration may not guarantee effective implementation, but it can alleviate your doubts. You can rest secure in the knowledge that you did, in fact, create this plan with others—that it's not just your own harebrained scheme—and you can take comfort in the shared accountability, knowing that you don't have to fight this battle entirely by yourself.

Focus on Progress, Not Success

Goals are great, but they sometimes trick us into all-or-nothing thinking: We've met the goal or we haven't. We're successes or we're failures. Regrettably, educational innovation often taunts us with such glittery visions of a reinvented school that we regard as failure anything less than instant transformation. To buck that trend, we must walk the razor's edge between painting an inspirational picture and being realistic about how long change actually takes. Inspire teachers with unrealistic ideas, and they'll come crashing down when the change process gets rocky. Share too much brutal reality up front, and they won't have the endurance to try. Teachers who have been through one change cycle after another grow exhausted, if not downright cynical, for this very reason: Leaders promise massive gains, and teachers feel like failures when the gains are modest. If, like me, you can't blame teachers for their skepticism, you're wondering how to keep your doubt, guilt, and fear under control as you find a balance between inspiration and reality.

For your sake and that of your staff, focus more on making progress and less on achieving goals. Progress keeps up team morale and, just as importantly, buoys your own confidence throughout the often turbulent change process. Focus on the "small wins." Celebrating any progress, no matter how minor, will keep wind in your sails and motivate the crew to keep working. The ancillary benefit is the mitigation of your own doubts. Seeing your innovations bearing fruit will overpower the discouraging voices in your head.

Identify *progress* as the most salient concept during your initial rollout. Don't let the ever-venerable SMART goals be the only topic of conversation; talk about moving the needle on student learning, behavior, or well-being. Talk about how *more* of whatever you're aiming for will help in and of itself. *More* freshmen on track? Great! *More* parents attending conferences? Awesome! Remind your team of the adage "Don't let the perfect be the enemy of the good." This will help you walk the fine line between idealism and reality. A leader who says, "We can't do everything perfectly, but we can do some things really well" is more likely to garner buy-in from teachers than one who promises immediate utopia.

Focusing on progress, as opposed to all-or-nothing success, also allows you to explain to staff how you will adjust the plan along the way if necessary. When the inevitable "Yeah, but" questions pour in, you can explain that if you're not making progress partway through the year, you'll adjust the plan. This can do wonders for your doubts (and theirs). First, you know you have options in case the plan is ineffective; if you're not making progress, you can course-correct. You also have a reasonable response to staff resistance. You're letting progress—not teacher attitude—be the determining factor, which suggests that you're neither a pushover nor an implacable tyrant. "Let's give it a try and see how it goes" is a much more palatable message to give—and receive—than "The decision has been made, and this conversation is over."

Teachers will appreciate knowing how you're measuring the plan's efficacy, and if you keep coming back to progress throughout the year, they will stay motivated as the metrics (hopefully) improve. If the metrics don't improve and you must adjust the plan, they'll value your flexibility and transparency, not to mention the respect you're showing them by not forcing ineffective methods on them.

Set Clear Expectations

Somewhere on your shelf is an entire book on change theory that explains, in excruciating detail, how to transform your team's mindset and behavior by setting clear expectations for staff. This isn't that book. Here, we're just talking about maintaining your confidence through the transformation process, and the rockiest part of that transformation comes when you lay down the law. Aspire to change hearts and minds first if you like, but sooner or later, you're going to have to hold people accountable. When you do, doubt will traipse in, making you feel like a brutal dictator. You will always have a few people who will test the limits, falling short on their responsibilities just to see what you'll do. You know, too, that some will disregard your expectations out of spite; they hate your innovations, and they simply refuse to comply.

To mitigate your doubt, focus on making your expectations crystal clear. The clearer you've been with staff, the more justified you will feel in upholding requirements. The goal of clarity compels you to zoom in on exactly what you want from your team, when you want it, and how you will monitor it. For example, Priya might say, "I want all lessons to start with a bellringer, right from the first day of school, and that's why I will do most of my walk-throughs at the start of each period." She is making her expectations abundantly clear. She's not relying on sweeping philosophical generalizations such as "I want lessons to be engaging" or "I believe in equity for all students." Noble though those sentiments may be, they are convictions, not expectations, and they could be interpreted differently by every staff member. Clearly communicated expectations leave no room for interpretation and no way to opt out.

Clear expectations also give you a clean conscience. You know without a doubt that you have outlined specific actions for your team. You stated these in person and in writing, and you answered their (worthy) questions. If they needed support to meet your expectations, you've provided it. What you have not done is mince your words to palliate their anxiety. You haven't caused confusion by hedging or rolling back your requirements, and you haven't muddied the waters by making exceptions. You were clear, and as Brené Brown says, "Clear is kind. Unclear is unkind" (Brown, 2018). She links this to the idea of accountability:

> Feeding people half-truths or bull**** to make them feel better (which is almost always about making ourselves feel more comfortable) is unkind. Not getting clear with a colleague about your expectations because it feels too hard, yet holding them accountable or blaming them for not delivering is unkind. (p. 48)

If you embrace the idea that "clear is kind," setting expectations for your staff starts to feel fair and ethical rather than mean and tyrannical. You're making sure your team knows what to do to be successful, and you're treating them like professionals who can and will meet your expectations. When you discover someone has fallen short of the requirement, you can explore what's holding them back, confident it isn't due to your own shortcomings.

Master Your Fear

The unofficial motto of the U.S. Marines is "Improvise, adapt, and overcome," the idea being that Marines trust their skills in the face of the unknown. Channel these elite warriors whenever you roll out an innovation. Even though you don't know what will happen, what hurdles you'll face, or what results you'll see, you must master your fear as you enter the unknown.

The key to mastering your fear is changing your self-image. Do you see yourself as the only brain in the room, the only advocate for change, the only source of innovation? Do you expect to have an answer to every question and a solution to every problem? Do you, in fact, make it your business to solve other people's problems for them? Well-meaning leaders do this all the time. They distort Truman's "The buck stops here" aphorism, interpreting it to mean that solid leadership requires omniscience, and burn themselves out trying to know and control everything. Ironically, this mentality stokes fear rather than allaying it because it's a fool's errand: We can't know and control everything, and in trying to, we inevitably fail, thus inflaming our doubt.

Instead of pressuring yourself to be all-knowing and all-powerful, try seeing yourself as a learner. Brené Brown's work is again helpful. As she says, "When we dare to lead, we don't pretend to have the right answers; we stay curious and ask the right questions" (Brown, 2018, cover copy). Or, in the immortal words of Ted Lasso: "Be curious, not judgmental" (Sudeikis et al., 2020).

If you cast yourself as curious, you will never fear the unknown. Curious people *love* the unknown. They want to swim around in it, basking in fresh discoveries and soaking in new knowledge. They believe confronting the unfamiliar helps them grow wiser and more capable. They're not reckless—they don't rush in with brazen bravado—but they know their skills are always evolving, preparing them to respond to whatever they discover in the vast unknown.

Many educational leaders view themselves this way—in theory, at least. The phrase "lifelong learner" is bandied around so often as to be meaningless, and I've never interviewed a job candidate who didn't proclaim a humble eagerness to learn. In practice, though, it's a different story. When trying to sell a plan in the face of implacable resistance, we often revert to a feral state, projecting invulnerability as a defense mechanism. We forget those noble intentions of curiosity and lifelong learning and pressure ourselves to have all the answers.

If you're looking to become the curious learner you aspire to be, focus on three habits of mind:

1. **See others as intelligent.** Liz Wiseman defines "multipliers" as leaders who "assume that people are smart and will figure it out. To their eyes, their organization is full of talented people who are capable of contributing at much higher levels" (Wiseman, 2017, p. 19). How might you lead your team when you truly believe them to be smart, talented, and capable of much more than you're currently asking of them? How might your responses to resistance, nitpicking, and manipulation be different?

You'd definitely spend less time solving other people's problems for them, and you'd probably discover latent leadership skills in otherwise quiet staff members. If you assume that other people are intelligent and capable of figuring out solutions on their own, you'll be less likely to frame yourself as the only innovator in the building, responsible for the success, happiness, and efficacy of every person in it.

2. **Ask an extra question.** When leaders project omniscience or invulnerability, it's often the result of speaking too quickly. We think, *Someone is bringing a problem to my attention—I must solve it immediately or I'm a terrible leader!* But we cannot solve problems if we don't have all the facts. To be truly curious, you must assume you *don't* know everything and explore the situation until you do. Commit to withholding your answers, advice, or ideas until you have asked one more question than you think you need to. When you feel yourself bursting to jump into a conversation with your sage advice, count to three in your head, form a question intended to deepen your understanding, and ask it. You—and your team—will be glad you took the time to understand before rushing in with a decision.

3. **Practice saying, "I don't know."** Embracing uncertainty is yet another virtue leaders *think* they embrace much more than they do. In the heat of the moment, when we're under pressure to answer rapid-fire questions and defend unpopular choices, we pop out answers without thinking through ramifications, often resorting to speculation, guesswork, or half-truths. Avoid this tendency by practicing ways to say, "I don't know" that sound natural

to you. This is easy for small-scale questions that have a definitive right answer: "That's a great question, and I want to make sure I'm giving you the right answer, so let me get back to you." It's harder when questions arise to which there can never be a solid, universal answer—when people ask you to predict the future, control the uncontrollable, or account for every hypothetical. Think about how to phrase an answer that essentially comes down to "I don't know" in a way that is conscientious, respectful, and honest. For example, if a teacher asks Priya how parents will respond to the new discipline policy—a question only a mind reader could answer—she can say, "All we can do is communicate clearly, which we have done, and uphold our policies consistently, which we will do. I don't know how parents will respond, and I can't control their reaction. I do know, though, that we will seek their perspective after we've tried the new policy for a semester."

Habits of mind that take us from omniscient overlord to curious learner mitigate our fear by helping us embrace the unknown. When facing a future that we can't predict or control, we want to feel confident in our ability to learn on the spot, assess the facts, and trust our teammates—in short, to improvise, adapt, and overcome.

In Summary

As thrilling as it feels initially, change leadership has a way of devolving into a fear factory. You have to sell a vision to teachers who have seen one leader after another introduce grand plans, battle staff resistance, and fizzle out. You can't blame them, but you also know you need to give your innovation your absolute best effort. Your job depends on making at least some progress, and you're hoping you can do so without damage to your relationships with teachers or, frankly, your sanity. This chapter is by no means a comprehensive manual to leading lasting innovations in your school or district; it is merely a set of techniques you can use to address the doubts you experience as you try to roll out change. Every time you talk about your change plan, be sure to **sell the collaboration as much as the plan** so that staff understand it was a group effort, not your own private scheme. **Focus on progress, not success**, which will increase morale and buy-in. **Set clear expectations** so you can simultaneously measure your team's progress and hold everyone accountable. Finally, **master your fear** by accepting that you can't see the future or control all the circumstances, and it's perfectly OK.

2

The Empty Empathizer

Just once, Davonte would like to reach the end of the day as principal at a high school without breaking up a student altercation. Hearing the call for help in the science hall, he sighs and heads on over, expecting yet another shoving match involving a cluster of excitable 9th grade boys.

What he sees is something else altogether. Jackson, a frequent flier in the dean's office, has Mr. Casey in a chokehold, his arm wrapped around the teacher's neck in a wrestling grip. The security guards shout for the fight to stop but are otherwise idle. Davonte intervenes, pulling Jackson away from Mr. Casey, who stands up, sputtering and choking. Apoplectic with rage, Mr. Casey screams at the student, "You f***ing waste of space! You belong in jail!" He then turns on the security guards and curses their helplessness with another gush of profanity. Finally, he yells at Davonte, "You don't give a f*** about our safety at all, do you? You sit on your fat ass all day while these delinquents attack teachers, you stupid mother f*****!"

Davonte snaps.

"Shut your mouth right now!" he bellows, abandoning all restraint. "How dare you talk to your students and colleagues like that? Do you know what I do all day? I clean up after you. I deal with the kids you can't control, the ones you send out of your room because you have the worst behavior management in the school. If they didn't hate you so much, maybe you wouldn't have found yourself in a chokehold!"

Davonte knows his outburst is wrong, but he also knows his perspective is right. The teacher has just cursed out a student, security guards, and his own boss in the middle of a crowded hallway. *What kind of idiot does that?* he wonders. *If he'd just kept his mouth shut, he would have been the innocent victim. But he had to blow his stack, and now I have to clean up his mess yet again.*

Several other administrators belatedly enter the scene and make moves to separate the explosive group, ferrying Mr. Casey to the nurse's office and Jackson to the dean's. Davonte doesn't talk to Mr. Casey or the security guards again that day, figuring everyone needs some time to cool off . . . especially him.

Over dinner that night, Davonte processes the situation. "Everyone was in the wrong," he tells Carla, his wife. "A student assaulted a teacher, security guards stood by, and the teacher cussed everyone out. What's wrong with these people? What's wrong with me? Don't I run a tighter ship than that?"

"What *is* wrong with you?" Carla asks, gently but honestly. "Why on earth did you lose it? Couldn't you see Mr. Casey was terrified and angry after what happened with Jackson? Of course he screamed at everyone. I'm not saying it was right, but it's a pretty human thing to do."

"I guess I just snapped. I've been dealing with Mr. Casey's garbage all year, and I hated watching him scream and curse at students. Maybe it's wrong of me, but I have zero sympathy for that little weasel. I'm human, too."

Carla winks. "You're not human, you're an administrator," she laughs. "You're supposed to be above all that."

She's right, of course. As a school leader, Davonte is supposed to be the steady center, keeping his composure when others act out. He's also supposed to have the emotional intelligence to empathize with people who have undergone trauma, stress, or physical danger, but he just can't right now. He's not sure how he'll be able to look Mr. Casey in the eye without shouting again, let alone rebuild the relationship. And the security guards—he'll have to deal with them, too, and try not to erupt in anger over the outright dereliction of their duty. Davonte goes to bed dreading the next day, when he will have to attempt to empathize with adults for whom he currently has nothing but scorn.

Debrief the Doubts

As a leader, your job is to work with people, and people are complex. In fact, they can be downright unreasonable, irrational, and self-centered. This can make empathizing one of the toughest aspects of leadership. No matter how friendly and compassionate you are, other people's problematic behavior sometimes gets in the way.

It's one thing to deal with the minor annoyances that are part of every administrator's life: difficult parents, bickering employees, misbehaving students. You gradually develop reliable responses and a robust set of tools for building relationships in the face of human fallibility. It's another thing entirely to encounter behavior so vile, so extreme, that it overwhelms your best practices and slaughters your empathy altogether. These moments are dangerous. Any uncharitable thoughts and intolerant impulses we normally keep at bay threaten to break through our otherwise calm exterior—and sometimes they actually do, landing us in hot water.

My career has not been without moments when my empathy came up short. I once broke up a fight between parents—parents!—while thinking, *I see where your kids get it, you terrible excuses for mothers.* Another time, I was physically repulsed to learn that a colleague, someone I used to like and respect, had crossed a boundary with a student. I even witnessed a student throwing a desktop computer at a dear teacher friend of mine and braced myself to do anything at all to stop the student from hurting her, even if it meant losing my job. From that moment on, I saw the student as a threat. In these extreme situations, I thought, *Nope. I can't do this. I can't be the emotionally steady pillar. Forget empathy; I'll never be able to look at these people with anything other than rage.* My anger and disgust threatened to overpower me, and I desperately wanted to lash out and say what I was really thinking. I wondered if I was going to be chronically infuriated for the rest of my career and feared how my strong emotions would affect my personal life.

When it comes to empathy, there's a huge gap between theory and practice. It's easy to consider hypothetical situations and other people's stories with saintly patience, but it's hard to be so virtuous in real life. If you side with Carla as she tries to help Davonte empathize with Mr. Casey, you probably have generous instincts. You try to look at tough situations from all perspectives and act rationally and kindly.

But just out of curiosity, have you ever snapped? Maybe you lost it during a crisis, as Davonte did, or maybe someone you secretly disliked just pushed one button too many and you bit his head off, damaging the relationship with a single careless response. Are there people who have forever lost your good opinion because of their repellent behavior? Do you view them with disdain and mistrust, even years after their transgression?

If we're being honest, all of us could answer at least one of these questions in the affirmative, despite our virtuous intentions. When we're challenged to respond with empathy to situations displaying the worst aspects of humanity, good intentions can go out the window. We may intellectually understand the baggage other people carry—trauma, fear, or special circumstances—but emotionally, we react with contempt. Such moments make us doubt whether we're really suited for leadership. *Am I a terrible person?* you might wonder. *Why am I so filled with anger and scorn? I'm supposed to be calm and understanding. Why can't I see this other person's perspective? Why do I want nothing more than to unleash my fury on them?* You realize you're falling short of the high bar leaders set for themselves and that you are not, in fact, unshakably forgiving and effortlessly empathetic, no matter how much you try to be. This makes you wonder if you even want to stay in leadership. *Why bother dealing with all this drama,* you think, *since I'm not cut out for this anyway?*

You know that you need to respond to such situations appropriately—after all, you are the professional leader—but your own heated emotions and the other person's shocking offenses create a lot of opportunity for error. The stakes here can be extremely high. One slip of the tongue and you could end up inflaming the situation, crossing an ethical or legal boundary, or getting into professional trouble. The front pages of local newspapers are strewn with school leaders who responded poorly to unsettling situations, including over- or underempathizing with those involved. Cut someone too much slack and you may turn a blind eye to serious offenses; come down too hard and you are painted as an unreasonable bully.

It doesn't help that, at the end of the day, you're human—which means you, too, can be unreasonable, irrational, and self-centered. So how do you overcome these challenges to find empathy for unreasonable, irrational, self-centered people who make you doubt your desire—let alone your ability—to stay in leadership?

Avoid the Pitfalls
Don't Open Your Mouth Until You Can Control What Comes Out of It

You likely get plenty of practice in carefully monitoring your speech, what with the tense meetings and tricky conversations that you encounter as part of your work. You know how to keep your thoughts to yourself. Some situations, however, have an insidious way of erasing what we know:

- Someone attacking us directly, screaming or cursing at us, can make us desperate to defend ourselves, perhaps deploying a few choice words in the process.
- An angry group of people, whom we normally like, ganging up on us can cause our temper to flare up and initiate "fight or flight" mode before we even realize it.
- Someone under our supervision doing something exceptionally dangerous, foolish, or unethical can trigger our instinct to react quickly and dramatically—and perhaps without considering consequences.

No matter how well we normally control ourselves, certain situations test our abilities. In the heat of the moment, when our emotions threaten to overpower us, we yearn to say the first thing to pop into our head—nearly always a mistake.

When you find yourself tempted to lash out, remember this: It's better to remain silent than to say something that will hurt you, and you know what will hurt you. If you attack, threaten, or swear, or if you appear to have lost control of your behavior, you will do direct, possibly irreparable, damage to yourself. If you can't think of anything else to say besides the rage-filled sentence on the tip of your tongue, keep your mouth firmly shut. People might think you're weak; let them. They might think you're stupid; you're not. On the contrary, it takes strength and intelligence to remain silent when your instinct is to say harsh things.

The faster your heart is beating, the slower your mouth should be moving. As your blood boils and your brain races with snappy retorts, take a deep breath and clamp your jaw shut until you have mastered any unsavory impulses.

Don't Throw Your Authority Around, Even When Provoked

You don't strut through the school saying, "I'm an administrator. Do what I say!" on a daily basis, and you don't need to do it in most extreme situations. If you're breaking up a lunchroom fight, announcing that you're the principal might help. If, on the other hand, you're working with a teacher who just violated the law, reminding them of your positional authority won't help the situation and will likely make it worse. Likewise, when you're dealing with irate parents at a child's expulsion hearing, there's no need to exercise your power—trust me, they know you're an authority figure.

We often want to remind volatile people of our authority because we believe it will curb their poor behavior. It won't. Someone engulfed in rage, fear, or other extreme emotions doesn't care that you're their boss. They're not going to be so awestruck in your presence that they suddenly control themselves. Look at Mr. Casey. He *wanted* to let Davonte have it. If Davonte had said, "Hold on there, buddy, I'm your boss," he would have looked like a pompous blowhard, and Mr. Casey would have cursed at him regardless.

When tempted to throw your power into the face of a difficult person, ask yourself what you're trying to achieve. Do you want to intimidate this person into submission? Are you hoping to get out of having a tough conversation? If so, don't do it. You're going to hurt your cause in the long run.

Don't Try to Solve Everything All at Once

One of the many reasons our empathy vanishes in extremely tense situations is sheer exhaustion: We know it will take days, weeks, or even months to resolve the problem (assuming resolution is possible), and that doing so will drain our last drop of tolerance. Take Davonte's incident. He has three separate issues on his hands: the student's violence, the teacher's outburst, and the security guards' neglect. He'll have to talk to each party separately, exerting all of his patience as he tries to redress the poor behavior while showing empathy. Then, too, there's the sheer complexity of the relationships involved; Mr. Casey and Jackson obviously have some underlying issues that need careful navigation, and Davonte would be foolish to simply reprimand them and walk away.

In your exasperation, you might be tempted to try solving all problems at once, eager to move past them. Although you can and should defuse people's heated emotions during a tense moment, you simply cannot bring a volatile situation to a true resolution until you've calmed everyone down, listened to their perspectives, and planned a reasonable response. Most of the time, poor behavior—including that of adults—is a cover for a deeper issue, so give yourself time to unearth what's really going on.

If you rush to solve all problems immediately, you will miss something. You'll make a decision with incomplete information, or you'll disregard someone's emotions and damage the relationship. As Brené Brown says, "Leaders must either invest a reasonable amount of time attending to fears and feelings, or squander an unreasonable amount of time trying to manage ineffective and unproductive behavior" (Brown, 2018, p. 67). So fight the urge to bring problems to a speedy solution and take the time to untangle them thread by thread.

Navigate a Path
Start with the Facts

If you're struggling to get your own feelings under control—to be the bigger person, the steady center, the empathetic leader—here's a simple first step: Focus on the facts. Of course, you will eventually want to rebuild relationships by demonstrating true empathy and attending to fears and feelings, but when that goal seems unattainable, start by collecting and organizing the facts of the situation. You can do this even when your insides are twisted in rage, fear, or disgust.

Think about the last time you broke up a fight, dealt with a bully, or confiscated a vape pen. You probably followed a protocol of dispassionately gathering facts and organizing information to resolve the issue. These skills may feel distant and irrelevant in the face of extreme behavior, but they can be a lifesaver. After all, if you're busy collecting facts, you're *not* losing your temper, cowering in fear, or recoiling in disgust. Rather, you're doing your job.

Your antagonists probably will not care about facts. They'll have abandoned themselves to their feelings, which is how everything started. In Davonte's predicament, Jackson assaulted a teacher and is in the throes of some drastic upheaval. Mr. Casey is screaming and cursing at his colleagues and the student—clearly, something inside him has broken. When people are overpowered by emotion, they believe their actions are justified. They don't care about rules or consequences. Mr. Casey may go to his grave believing that Jackson *is* a waste of space who should be in jail, and that Davonte *is* a stupid—well, you get the idea. If he faces disciplinary action, he will simply take it as a sign of a crooked system, not a consequence of his own poor decisions.

Focusing on the facts helps you, the leader, untangle such situations, even when your ability to empathize is under attack. Those involved will clamor to explain why: *why* they acted out, *why* their actions are justified, *why* the other person deserves immediate condemnation. Don't let them suck you in, at least not while your own emotions are raging. You don't want to engage in a discussion about whether bad behavior is justified while you are off-kilter. For now, focus on the *who, what,* and *when*. This will help you engage with the situation without losing your cool. It will also help you turn the discussion to natural consequences; for example, physical violence may result in medical intervention or a report to police. As consequences ensue, the offending parties may begin to think about something other than their stormy emotions.

Focusing on the facts is simple but not always easy. Ask any leader who has had to look into a colleague's eyes and ask a clarifying question that sums up unsavory facts.

- "And was that when you yelled the N-word?"
- "Three staff members say you dragged a student down the hall by the hair. Did you?"
- "Did you use your district-issued device to send that inappropriate picture to Abby?"

Your poker face might fail you as you drill down to the truth—I know I've struggled to keep my hands and voice from shaking as I worked through extreme scenarios—but remember that your goal isn't to *feel* a certain way, it's to *act* professionally: to ask thorough questions, to record accurate facts, and to give all parties the opportunity to contribute. You can do all of these things even while feeling nervous or judgmental.

Look at it this way: You will never be reprimanded for having a shaky voice or clenched jaw while collecting a witness's statement, as long as your words and actions are professional. But shouting, threatening, cursing, blustering, slamming doors, and generally losing it will earn you a reprimand. When you feel tempted to engage in less-than-professional behavior, divert your attention to the concrete task of fact collection. Not only is it more productive than ranting and raving, but it also gives you time to cool off as you consider your next steps.

Find One Area of Understanding

Good news! The people involved in a contentious situation will probably line up outside your office to explain their perspective and enlist your empathy. They *want* you to validate their reasons for behaving unreasonably and irrationally. They're going to drown you in details, piling on more and more information, so you will see that they have not, in fact, been self-centered at all. You probably won't have to work hard to gather everyone's perspective.

Here's the bad news: Your brain will interpret a lot of this information as desperate excuse-making. Mr. Casey's side of the story, for example, sounds to Davonte like a petulant, ineffective teacher scrambling to justify wildly inappropriate behavior. You might also get hung up on the fact that, even if you could empathize with someone's perspective, it doesn't change the hard facts of the situation or diminish the consequences. For example, no matter how eagerly Jackson might try to justify his behavior to Davonte, he still assaulted a teacher, and no excuse is strong enough to keep him out of serious trouble.

That's why it's essential to understand the difference between empathizing and excusing. Empathizing says, "Your feelings are valid" while excusing says, "Your actions are valid." When we struggle to empathize, it's often because we view empathy as the gateway to leniency—show a little compassion, and next thing you know, the school will be an apocalyptic free-for-all, overrun with marauding hooligans. This all-or-nothing attitude is both shortsighted and damaging to ourselves. You will never be truly empathetic if you're afraid of appearing too soft, so you need to delineate between showing compassion and making excuses. You must develop the ability to, as the saying goes, "hate the sin, love the sinner."

Give yourself permission to empathize without fear of being lax. When those involved in a confrontation pour out their harrowing epics, listen for one feeling you can identify with. You have certainly felt fear, anger, pride, and so many other emotions that cause people to behave poorly, so listen for these as they unload their stories. Beware, however, of the temptation to compare your own behavior with that of others. "I've been angry, but I've never punched anyone . . . unlike you!" is not an empathetic response. You don't want to hold yourself up as a role model, you want to present yourself as a fellow human. "I know what it's like to be angry" is a solid start—even if that's all you can manage without veering into judgmental moralizing. The first step to effective empathy is to communicate understanding of another person's feelings, even if you don't approve of their actions.

Reflect Your Way into Emotional Intelligence

You've stayed cool while collecting the facts, and you've found at least one area of understanding with someone who's behaved badly. But you're still seething with rage, impatience, and contempt. You're still doubting your own ability to be an empathetic leader, an emotionally steady pillar. You fear you're turning into a cynical, angry crank, and you wonder why you don't have the emotional intelligence to weather these storms with grace.

To develop that emotional intelligence, you must practice humble, continual, conscientious reflection. This is yet another ideal we theoretically espouse but ignore in practice because, of course, we get caught up in the heat of the moment. Confronted with someone else's cruelty or selfishness—not to mention our own impatience and anger—it's hard to process the situation as a learning experience, but this is precisely what we must do. Other people will always be unreasonable, irrational, and self-centered, but we can get better at responding to them if we are willing to ask ourselves the right questions and answer them honestly.

The first question to ask yourself is *What am I feeling and why?* This is more complicated than it sounds. Our instinct is to ignore feelings we perceive as shameful, such as fear, doubt, or embarrassment, so we often mislabel them as feelings we cast as virtuous, such as righteous anger. Take Davonte, for instance. He might state, "I'm feeling angry because Mr. Casey is an idiot," but that's an oversimplification. Yes, he's angry, but he's also feeling *embarrassed* that a teacher under his wing acted so poorly, *guilty* about not building a stronger relationship with Mr. Casey, *sad* for the student who received the teacher's outburst, and *exhausted* at the prospect of cleaning up the whole mess. Acknowledging all these feelings is the first step on the path to developing emotional intelligence.

When you answer the *why* part of this question, focus on yourself—do not blame other people for "making" you feel a certain way. "Jackson and Mr. Casey made me angry," Davonte might think, but that is simply not true. No one can *make* you feel anything. That's why another administrator could face Davonte's predicament but feel perfectly calm and collected. As Marcus Aurelius said, "If you are distressed by anything external, the pain is not due to the thing itself, but to your estimate of it, and this you have the power to revoke at any moment." In other words, you choose your reaction. Deny this fact, and you rob yourself of the chance to make better choices. Acknowledge it, and you have the power to stop certain emotions in their tracks. So, as you reflect on your feelings, try to do so without blaming others for them. You might come up against some truths you can confess only to yourself, such as the following:

- *I'm feeling fearful because if I handle this wrong, I could end my career.*
- *I'm feeling embarrassed that I shouted, so I'm covering it up with righteous indignation.*
- *I'm frustrated and regretful because I chose a job where I am continually screamed at.*

The second question to ask is *What are these feelings doing to me?* Chances are, your answer to this question will be unsettling—after all, you're doubting yourself. You feel so much anger, fear, impotence, jealousy, hopelessness, and other poisonous emotions that you know something is wrong. Still, you have to spell it out:

- *My anger is damaging my relationships with colleagues.*
- *My frustration makes every day at work torture.*
- *My embarrassment is preventing me from putting myself out there.*

Putting the truth into words forces you to reckon with the consequences of indulging certain emotions. You can *choose* better emotional reactions in response to comprehending the damage you do to yourself when you respond with anger, fear, and other toxic feelings. Internalize the fact that these emotions hurt you more than they hurt anyone else; then, and only then, will you be able to stop them in their tracks.

Finally, ask, *What feelings do I want to replace these toxic feelings?* Maybe you want to feel a sense of belonging, pride in your work, or composure during chaos. Dwell on these aspirations. Think about how they will help you become the leader you want to be, even when others aren't the people you wish they were. Once you define the emotions you aspire to instead of poisonous ones, find ways to practice them daily. For example, if you want to be a calming presence during extreme crises, practice being calm during petty scuffles. Focus on keeping your voice steady, your body loose, and your head clear. Then, when you find yourself in an intensified, even shocking, situation, you will be able to draw on muscle memory and a clear vision of who you want to be in heated moments.

Emotionally intelligent self-talk in response to an extreme situation might sound like this: *I have the power to choose my response. I can let fear, anger, or disgust overpower me, or I can choose to be a force for good, no matter what. I can acknowledge the atrocities before me without letting them determine my emotions.*

You're not going to get it right every time. This is where reflection comes in. After every situation that calls on you to face down other people's bad behavior, reflect on your own. What feelings did you choose, what did they do to you, and how close are you to being the leader you want to be? Though sometimes painful, reflection is the only way to grow. The wise, unshakable veterans you admire, the ones who confidently weather even the most litigious clashes, got where they are by reflecting after every core-shaking encounter. They screwed up again and again. Like you and me, they sometimes lost control, damaged relationships, and spent sleepless nights agonizing over how to respond to the challenging people they work with. Their composure was forged through years of careful reflection.

The doubt we feel in extreme situations typically springs from our own off-kilter emotions. We feel out of control, out of our depth, or plumb out of empathy. That's why any effort to face these situations with confidence necessarily entails developing emotional intelligence, which will allow us to manage our own feelings and respond well—and even empathetically—to others' feelings.

In Summary

Inevitably, you will face appalling, confidence-shaking crises as a direct result of other people's wrongdoing. Some veterans will advise you to "develop a thick skin" to allow violence, cruelty, neglect, selfishness, or caprice to roll right off you. But before you exchange your skin for scales, think it through: Is that who you want to be? For me, the answer is no. I never want to be the sort of person who *isn't* horrified when, for example, a student hits a teacher, but I also don't want to be so shaken that I leave the profession. I want to have the skills to respond confidently and appropriately. The long journey to becoming this person begins with a simple step: **Start with the facts.** Approach them with neutrality as you and others review them. When you're not sure how to wrangle your tempestuous emotions, **find one area of understanding** and use it for, if not empathy, at least compassion. Finally, **reflect your way into emotional intelligence** by embracing your own role in the situation and remembering that you can choose your emotional responses.

3

The Punching Bag

"Come to my office, right now."

Carlos is a district-level director, but as he registers the command, he feels like an errant kindergartner. Scurrying to his boss's office, he wonders what on earth he's done now. The last time those six words showed up in his texts, they foreshadowed a tirade enumerating his various failures and leaving him feeling as though he had single-handedly polluted the learning of every child in the district. Maybe today he'll be accused of foolishness, inaction, or some other defect—he's heard it all, usually tinted with an impressive palette of profanity. It's no surprise, therefore, that the rant begins the moment he enters the office of Debra, his boss.

Carlos has known Debra for a decade, and this is just how it is. Debra will hear something on the grapevine—Carlos didn't prepare proper training, Carlos was inconsiderate during a meeting, Carlos's team isn't moving in the right direction—and explode. The weird thing is that Carlos knows he can't be doing *that* terribly. Debra hires him back every year and has even promoted him twice. She gives Carlos autonomy over projects and holds him up as an example for others. The two have hours-long coaching sessions, and Carlos can confidently call Debra a mentor, and sometimes even a friend.

Ironically, Carlos has been the friend Debra turns to after being raked over the coals by her own boss, the superintendent. He's talked Debra off the proverbial ledge as, choking back tears, she recounted a harrowing outburst from someone who could endanger her career with one angry swoosh. Sometimes Carlos wonders if Debra sees anything contradictory in her behavior—recoiling from the superintendent's rages one minute, blowing up at her subordinates the next—but it doesn't seem like it. As far as Carlos can tell, administrators just yell at each other. They can't yell at students, parents, or teachers, so they vent their spleen on the one person who has to sit there and take it: the person right below them on the leadership pyramid.

Still, it's nerve-wracking. Carlos might go months without a dressing-down from Debra, but he knows that, eventually, he will make a mistake, someone will say something about him, or Debra will simply be in a vindictive mood, and he'll be thrown into a cycle of fear, anger, and atonement all over again. It's only a matter of time before he steps on one of the many land mines scattered around the office. It feels like he spends more time managing his professional relationship with Debra than he spends managing his actual work tasks.

Debrief the Doubts

Carlos is right about one thing: Being yelled at is an inevitable part of the job. You work with parents, students, teachers, union leaders, board members, and a whole pile of administrators who outrank you. Right or wrong, some of them are going to blow up at you. It feels more manageable when you're working with an angry student, teacher, or even a parent, because you're in control of the situation and you know how to defuse it. It's quite different when the person unleashing their fury has the power to fire you.

A boss's outburst can unleash a flood of doubt. If you're completely caught off guard by the accusations leveled against you, you might wonder whether you're out of touch, obliviously failing everyone and everything. Or perhaps you'll descend into paranoia, believing yourself trapped in a web of spies who gleefully pour slander into your boss's ear. If the onslaught follows a genuine mistake, you might join in the castigation, cursing your incompetence and resigning yourself to a lifetime of mediocrity. If, on the other hand, you're being chastised unfairly, an elixir of anger and fear might start to poison you from the inside out, withering your trust, corroding your joy, and making every day feel like a fight to survive a toxic environment.

Secrecy, in the guise of professional discretion, makes the dysfunction all the worse. Leaders are supposed to conduct themselves with dignity and self-control, so they pretend that's what they do at all times. No one talks about screaming, threats, or mind games. Those on the receiving end of a leader's outbursts may be too confused or ashamed to discuss it with their colleagues—and even if they did, redress is unlikely. Unless the boss's language meets the human resources department's definition of abusive, it probably won't stand up to an official complaint. Administrators aren't covered by a union, so the right to a respectful work environment remains, sadly, theoretical. The "chain of screaming" (a theory propounded by character Barney Stinson in the television show *How I Met Your Mother* [Bays et al., 2008]) is all too often an endemic part of administrative life.

Funnily enough—or maybe not—no one ever admits to screaming at a colleague. I've known a Debra or two in my career, and they always excuse their outbursts as being "passionate." The ones with real chutzpah have told me, "That was nothing compared to what *my* boss put me through." Their explanations at times resemble language used by abusers: "Be grateful it wasn't worse"; "I put up with it and so can you"; or the classic "You're making me act like this." These excuses and the tirades that precede them can be particularly triggering if you've experienced abuse in the past. They might cause you to feel helpless, trapped, angry, and desperate to make it stop. You might detach, watching your boss's tantrum with cold contempt, wondering how a person with so little self-control ever became a leader. You might even fantasize about the day they'll get their well-deserved comeuppance.

Not all reprimands are abusive, nor are they all based on unfounded accusations. Sometimes, your boss yells because you messed up, they're having a bad day, or a hundred other reasons. You and I know that leaders need to find kinder ways to correct employees and healthier ways to release anger than pitching a fit, but until they do, you need to develop the ability to confidently respond to the situation in the heat of the moment. It's a tricky prospect: you obviously don't want to engage in outright combat by firing back, but immediate surrender often doesn't feel right either. So how do you stay confident when you are raked over the coals by the person who determines whether you keep your job?

Avoid the Pitfalls
Don't Assume Your Boss Is Entirely Wrong

It's easy to take constructive criticism when it's delivered by a caring, compassionate coach. It's harder to take when delivered by an angry, shrieking boss. That's why you might miss the nugget of truth hiding in the histrionics. You might be so infuriated at the unprofessional behavior of your boss that you immediately assume they're jumping to conclusions or spouting downright lies. Their rage sparks your rage, and you immediately go on the defensive, looking for context (dare I say excuses?) to respond with. It's a natural instinct to throw all blame on someone behaving like a maniac and reserve none for ourselves, but remember that more than one person can be at fault at a time.

Deplore your boss's behavior all you want, but their tantrum does not automatically exonerate you. Listen to what your boss is saying. Look for the facts—the fair accusations, the true failings, the ways in which you've come up short. Look, too, for perceptions, because in the hyperpolitical leadership arena, perception is often reality, and how you're seen can make or break your career. If you're giving off a certain vibe, or if people are getting the wrong impression, you need to know so that you can correct it. Collect facts and take note of perceptions so that you can craft a measured, thoughtful response to them once the initial confrontation ends. For now, though, quell the defensive, self-righteous internal voice telling you how blameless you are and listen for any truth behind the tantrum.

Don't Assume Your Boss Is Entirely Right

On the other hand, don't let yourself collapse into self-loathing the instant your boss starts their tirade. If they're describing real errors on your part, it's hard not to fall into the pit of despair. Maybe you screwed up big time, or maybe your boss is confronting you with a long line of mistakes you've made without realizing it. Perhaps you're learning for the first time how other people see you, and you're shocked at and ashamed of how you come across.

Facing brutal facts can make it easy to unravel, believing yourself to be the most incompetent leader ever to darken the school's doorway. You might, in fact, outdo your boss, hurling all manner of unsavory names and accusations at yourself. *I should just quit now*, you might think. *I'm not cut out for this.*

But don't jump into that pit just yet, even if—and especially if—your boss seems to want you to. Being unequivocally in the wrong in one particular situation doesn't make you a terrible person or a terrible leader. It makes you a person who made mistakes, just like everyone else. Look at it this way: You will never be a good leader if you believe you are horrible, because horrible people can't be good leaders. You have to give yourself grace, accept your own failures, and learn from them. There are usually mitigating factors even in the most egregious errors, and of course, we are more than our mistakes.

Don't React Emotionally

If you throw your own emotional fuel onto the fire, you're going to get burned. You might be seething with rage at the injustice of it all, but you must get a grip on your feelings. Mounting a heated defense—whether that means yelling back or ardently stating your position—will escalate the situation. You know this from your work with kids (your students and perhaps your own), yet it's hard to resist the urge to argue when under attack, particularly by someone you view as powerful, even invulnerable. Ultimately, though, arguing with your boss is going to have the exact same result as it would with anyone else: It will make the situation worse. Anger may provoke both of you to say things you'll regret and complicate any future reconciliation.

That doesn't mean you have to cower in fear. Fear may well be the dominant emotion in the moment, but try not to indulge in it during your boss's tirade. If you have experience with people who yell habitually, you know that crying, groveling, and apologizing do precisely nothing to allay anyone's rage. All you will achieve by cowering is to make your boss see you as weak. You might even start to believe it yourself. But you're not weak, and every minute you can hold back your tears, your panic, and your doomsday scenarios will prove it. Someone who chooses to display authority by forcing you to endure their blowup likely sees a link between an exercise of power and true internal strength, and they are looking for you to exhibit some fortitude. If you struggle to shelve your fear in the moment, remember this: The worst thing this person can do to you is fire you. They can't take your family, friends, or faith. They can't change who you are as a human. Chances are, they can't even damage your overall career that much—they may set it back a bit or force you to make a lateral move for a time, but education is a huge industry that is currently short on workers, including administrators. The reality is that you have plenty of opportunities, no matter your background. So stick it out and don't let your fear bubble over.

Navigate a Path

Express as Much Agreement as You Can

Agree on anything—*anything*—your conscience will allow. Agree on your boss's description of the problem, the context, the consequences, or even your own error. Agree on what's most important to do next. Heck, agree on the weather. When you agree with your boss, you're aligning with them. You're telling your boss, "You and I want the same things." You are, in other words, building a shared pool of understanding, which is the first step to de-escalating your boss's anger—and possibly your own.

It's easier to do this when your boss's accusations are at least partially valid. For example:

- "You know what, Debra, you're right. I must not have explained the policy to my department very well, and that's why three of my team members broke the rules last week."

- "Well, I definitely agree with you that the meeting was unproductive. I think there were a lot of reasons for this, but I'd like to acknowledge that my attitude was one of them."
- "It's absolutely true that the committee is heading in the wrong direction. Can we talk about some of the complicating factors that are slowing it down?"

It is harder, but even more essential, to find areas of agreement when your boss has the wrong idea and is attacking you with a barrage of false accusations. For example:

Debra: "I can't believe you didn't talk with your department about the new tech rollout! You've made us all look like a bunch of careless idiots!"

Carlos: "Debra, the tech rollout is so important to me and to my department. I know you and I both believe it has the power to change teaching and learning across our school. That's why I spent our entire December meeting going over those expectations with my team. Can I show you the agenda so we can make sure I was clear?"

* * *

Debra: "Erica says you completely blew up at her yesterday, and I'm so disgusted that you would treat a teacher like that."

Carlos: "Blowing up at a teacher is completely unacceptable. That's why I'd never do it. Like you, I believe that everyone deserves respect, and I'm so sorry to hear about Erica's perception of what happened. Can I share my account of the situation with you?"

* * *

Debra: "Why do you never keep me informed as to what's going on in your department?"

Carlos: "Debra, I think it's essential to keep you informed. I try very hard to do just that, but I'm obviously falling short somewhere. Can we go over what I've been doing, then discuss how I can do better?"

Note that you can find areas of agreement while still presenting your side of the story. You don't have to admit to something you didn't do, but you do have to demonstrate that you want what your boss wants: a smoothly functioning school. When you find areas of agreement, you communicate that you are rational and open to improvement. That's exactly what you need in this situation. If your boss is right and you messed up, you want to appear receptive to feedback rather than stubbornly defensive. If your boss is wrong and you're being falsely accused, you want to come across as levelheaded. That's the only way to plead your case, calm your boss down, and steer the conversation into productive territory.

Defusing your boss's fury by acknowledging areas of agreement also buys you time to consider your next steps. The more time you need, the more areas of agreement you should point out. Say, for instance, you're trying to find a way to mention the fact that your boss is partially at fault for the situation they're presently screaming about. You can't just say, "Look, you brought this on yourself." You need time to think about whether and how you'll bring up this potentially inflammatory topic. To buy yourself time, keep agreeing: "Yes, we need to build better relations with the board"; "It's true, we don't have many opportunities"; "I wish they knew more about our work as well"; and so on. With every agreement, your boss will cool down—the lack of resistance takes some steam out of the engine. As the conversation goes on, you can decide whether it's worth connecting your boss's past actions to the present problem.

Ask Yourself Why a Reasonable Person Would Act This Way

When someone acts atrociously, it's common to assume they are an atrocious person. The authors of *Crucial Accountability:*

Tools for Resolving Violated Expectations, Broken Commitments, and Bad Behavior coined the term "fundamental attribution error" to describe ascribing a person's misdeeds to some innate flaw in their character (Patterson et al., 2013). They suggest that, instead of indulging our belief that the other person is inherently awful, we should ask, "Why would a reasonable, rational, and decent person do that?" (p. 59).

Ranting and raving isn't a good look on anyone, so it can be hard to see a reasonable, rational, and decent person beneath all the fury. That doesn't mean there isn't one. Decent people do terrible things all the time, including losing their temper. Yes, some people do it more than others. No, it's not OK. Still, starting with the assumption that your boss is a reasonable person will help you navigate difficult conversations. Right off the bat, it will moderate your emotions. You may be violently angry, infuriated at the injustice, or disgusted by your boss's behavior, but if you see your boss as fundamentally decent, you will be more able to separate the sin from the sinner. When called to the boss's office, you may fear instant dismissal, but if you see the boss as reasonable and rational, you can shelve this fear and look for fair treatment.

Asking, "Why would a reasonable, rational, and decent person do that?" also invites you to consider your boss's perspective on a deeper level than whether they are right or wrong. Chances are, your first thoughts during a contentious conversation will involve several binary, moralistic judgments: *Are the accusations correct or incorrect? Were my own actions justified or not? Is my boss's behavior appropriate or hateful?* Instead of these, try asking, *Why is my boss acting like this?* which provides much more useful speculation. When you resist the temptation to ascribe your boss's actions to caprice, you may see other reasons for their behavior. Maybe your boss is under extreme pressure and threat of dismissal from their own boss, and your mistake has made things worse. Maybe your boss's mental focus is consumed by a difficult family situation, and every mistake made at work frays their nerves even more. Maybe every supervisor your boss ever had has yelled at employees, so this is the only way they know to redirect behavior.

Again, these are explanations, not justifications. Screaming, threatening, and accusing are still wrong, even when motivated by an understandable cause. That said, you will have an easier time relating to your boss if you can imagine why they're acting like this and empathize. Who among us hasn't snapped under pressure or vented anger at the first unlucky person to cross our paths? Who hasn't unthinkingly channeled the poor behavior of our parents or mentors? Who doesn't get angry when someone makes things worse for them?

When your boss is ranting at you, you might forget that you are allowed to ask questions, but asking questions during a confrontation can help you deduce why a reasonable, rational, decent person is currently acting so egregiously. The key is to appear concerned, not condescending. If you give the impression that you're trying to psychoanalyze your boss rather than address the problem, you'll make things worse. If, though, you ask relevant questions at the right time, you might be able to de-escalate the situation and learn more about your boss's emotional state. Focus on asking clarifying questions to enhance your overall understanding of your boss's perspective. Clarify the story: Who said what? When did they say it? What was the effect? Clarify the context: Why is this important? What has been happening all year that has made this issue so crucial? Clarify your boss's perspective: How does this impact them? Why are they so angry? Is it a case of wounded pride?

Obviously, unreasonable, irrational, terrible people do exist. I'm not saying that all bosses are automatically saints. I do, however, encourage you to look for an understandable explanation for your boss's behavior before writing them off as a despicable villain. Considering the possibility that your boss is fundamentally reasonable, rational, and decent will broaden your perspective while deepening your empathy, which can only help you as a leader.

Prioritize Fixing the Problem

Your boss believes you are in the wrong. That's the problem you need to fix. Whether or not the accusations leveled against you are justified, whether or not you could have prevented this situation, whether or not this was an innocent misunderstanding—none of it matters, at least not at first. Your boss believes you are in the wrong, and you need to fix that perception.

Some people find this a hard pill to swallow. They are so rankled by what they perceive as injustice, unable to move past unfair judgment, that they cannot compartmentalize the situation. They stew in self-righteousness, paralyzed by their own anger, and refuse to do what it takes to change their boss's perception. Here's the rough truth: Those people don't last long in their positions. I once knew an administrator whose boss told him repeatedly to spend more time in classrooms. The administrator insisted he simply couldn't do it because his schedule was so stuffed with meetings and people kept flowing into his office unannounced. I wanted to shake him. He was a high-level leader—he could have told his many direct reports never to drop in unexpectedly, he could have made his meetings more efficient or reduced their number, and he could have told his secretary to simply add classroom visits to his schedule and fend off anyone trying to horn in on that precious time. When I suggested these solutions to him, he balked, replying virtuously that he *wanted* to be available for his team, that he loved the amount of time they spent laughing and chatting in meetings. In his mind, he was a good leader whose boss just didn't understand the nature of his work.

He was fired later that year.

You must confront the reality that failure to fix your boss's perception can have serious consequences. You can be a conscientious, capable, diligent leader, but if your boss sees you as careless, incompetent, or lazy, your relationship will be fraught—and possibly short. That's why the first order of business is fixing the perception.

If your boss is bringing up valid problems with your performance, you can repair both perception and reality at once. The first step here is a no-brainer: Fix your shortcomings. Not visiting enough classrooms? Establish a weekly quota and meet it, no matter what. Not building enough relationships with the union? Get some collaborative meetings on the calendar, pronto. If you're open and determined, you already have everything you need to address the issue. Don't forget the crucial second step, though: Make sure your boss knows about your improvement. Make your boss abundantly aware of your effort to address the concerns raised. Do not fix the problem in secret, hoping word will reach your boss through divine intervention. Meticulously document your steps—meetings, strategies, and so on—and share them with your boss in the spirit of professional growth, then reflect together on your progress. Ask your boss how you're doing and solicit advice on how to continue to grow. Nothing exemplifies leadership better than using feedback as fuel for improvement. Be that kind of learning leader. You'll be glad you did, both because you'll be on a path to success and because you'll be able to look back and realize how much you evolved throughout the process.

If, on the other hand, you don't agree with your boss's accusations, you still have to fix the perception problem. This requires you to analyze the situation and strategize your response. Use the following questions to guide your thinking:

- **Analyze**—Where is your boss getting their information? Are they observing your actions firsthand or drawing conclusions from secondhand reports? Who is approaching your boss with comments about you? Whose word does your boss trust the most, and how much does your boss trust you?

  Strategize—Do everything possible to communicate about your work directly so your boss is not reliant on the grapevine. You do not want the perception of your work colored by other people's interpretation, whether they are maliciously gossiping or making innocent observations. Run ideas past your boss before you act on them. Invite your boss to your meetings and ask for feedback. Share drafts of your work to make sure you're on the right track. By bringing your boss into your work process, you minimize your chances of walking into a land mine and being surprised by an angry reaction to some misstep you made without knowing. You also increase your boss's trust by proving yourself to be transparent and open to guidance.

- **Analyze**—What's *really* going on with your boss, emotionally? Is their pride wounded over some setback in student performance? Are they straining under the pressure of union negotiations? Are they fearful of losing their own job?

Strategize—You might not be able to fix your boss's problems, but you can tailor your efforts to their needs. If your boss is going through tough times at home, for instance, find ways to lighten the load at work by handling extra tasks. If your boss is struggling to bargain with the union, present your ideas through the lens of workplace harmony. If your boss is afraid of being fired, learn about their high-stakes projects and support them in any way you can. If this sounds manipulative, ask yourself what you would want someone to do for you if you were in their shoes? If you were caring for a dying parent, for example, would you be angry to have your coworkers pitch in a bit more around the office? Of course not; you'd be grateful. Understanding your boss's emotional state can help you respond appropriately—not just with abstract empathy but with concrete actions.

- **Analyze**—What are your boss's top priorities? If the two of you disagree adamantly about the quality of your job performance, there's obviously a disconnect somewhere, and it's probably one of prioritization. Are you spending your time on the tasks your boss wants you to spend it on? Are you working toward the same goals?

    Strategize—You have to think flexibly. If your boss says something is important, you may have to realign your priorities, even if you disagree. It is, in fact, your boss's prerogative to establish which goals are most important. Try to look at the situation through your boss's lens, which is probably more panoramic than yours, to get a sense of why specific initiatives matter more than others. Don't forget that you can ask questions. If you disagree with what your boss wants you to focus on, you can tactfully ask for help understanding the rationale, the process, or what you're trying to achieve in the long run. You can't flout directives or ignore your boss's advice, but you are entitled to understand why you're doing what you're doing.

There's no simple process for changing your boss's perception, but change it you must. Fix your actual failures and use every tool in your kit to fix perceived ones. If you want to keep your job, you cannot die on the hill of your own self-righteousness, refusing to bend even an inch. You need to be adaptable, willing to see issues through your boss's eyes, and brave, willing to do things differently to close the gap between how your boss sees you and how you want to be seen.

Manage Up

If you have a humble, reflective boss who nurtures you, guides you, and makes every day at work a blissful partnership, never threatening or lashing out, I'm happy for you. The rest of us need to learn to "manage up." Even generally decent bosses are still people with their own quirks, biases, and, yes, faults. At some point, your boss is going to fall short of your expectations, just as you have sometimes fallen short of the expectations of those you lead. *Managing up* simply means building a strong enough relationship with your boss to know their needs, style, and preferences and adapt your behavior accordingly. Managing up is the best preventive measure you can take against future explosions.

As you get to know your boss, try to answer these essential questions:

- **Communication**—How much communication does your boss want from you? Do they want to know every last detail

of your work, or just the highlights? Do they prefer regular written reports or in-person meetings?
- **Decision making**—How involved does your boss want to be in your decision making? In which areas, if any, do you have sole control? Does your boss get irritated if you run ideas past them, or do they prefer to be in the loop?
- **Vision and goals**—What are your boss's goals, both for themselves and for the organization? Are they angling for a promotion? Do they see the team expanding in the future? How can you support these goals?

Carlos, from our vignette, should consciously cultivate a relationship with Debra, learning how she operates and what she expects from him. This will enable him to tailor his work to her style, communicating the way she wants and bringing her into his decision making. He can support her vision for the team and do what he can to further her professional aspirations. With every passing year, her trust in him will increase as he proves himself an adaptable, dependable, intelligent employee who can take direction. He, in turn, will be less and less likely to walk over some hidden land mine by failing in an area Debra deems important. He will go from punching bag to indispensable colleague.

Managing up is an essential skill even when you have a great boss. Let's talk, however, about bosses who are . . . less than great. The ones who are, in fact, straight-up awful—true abusers, manipulators, tyrants. They're out there, and maybe you've spent this whole chapter frustrated because no amount of empathy and adaptability can manage up to the belligerent bully currently signing your paychecks.

It's not as easy as simply leaving your job. You may have excellent reasons for sticking out an awful boss. Maybe the location, salary, workload, and promotional prospects of your job are all perfect, and this person is the fly in the ointment. Maybe you haven't been in your position very long, and if you leave now, it will look suspicious on a résumé. Maybe you've been trying desperately to get out but haven't received the right offer, so you're trapped for another year.

If you're intentionally sticking out a cruel, capricious boss, the best you can do is cope. This does not necessarily mean abandoning the idea of managing up and finding solace in dubious after-hours pleasures; you can and should find coping mechanisms at work. The most effective mechanism comes down to three crucial letters: CYA. You must cover your ... *assets* ... at all times. Build a fortress to protect yourself from the boss's caprice. I suggest a three-part armament: constant communication, rigorous documentation, and high political credit.

Constantly communicating with your tyrannical boss might be unpleasant, but it's the best weapon in your arsenal. Here's why: It renders your boss less likely to chastise you for acting against their wishes. You're showing your boss your plans, sharing drafts of your emails, running your ideas past them, calibrating your answers to tricky questions, asking for opinions on complex problems, and more. If you're a good actor, you can do this under the guise of wanting your boss's wise counsel, but really, you're protecting yourself from acting in a way that will run afoul of your boss.

This technique means nothing, however, unless you document everything—*everything*—and make sure the written record is stored where both you and your boss have access. Whatever you discuss during your meetings, take detailed notes in a cloud-based document so you can refer to it when your boss shifts the goalpost. Anytime you act based on your boss's guidance, make sure to send an email confirming the direction and referring to the conversation the two of you had. Paranoid? Maybe. Safe? Yes. Manage your boss's fluctuating nature by making sure all decisions, all strategies, all objectives are completely transparent and rigorously documented.

Your final weapon is to build your own political credit. This tool is less about managing your boss and more about understanding the ecosystem in which you work. If your boss runs hot and cold on you, consider how you can build steady credit in the form of admiration, trust, or public accolades. Turn your nose up on sordid politics if you like, but educational leadership is a political arena. I'm not talking about state and federal laws; I'm talking about the courtly intrigue that saturates even the smallest districts. You need to consider what you have going for you besides your boss's wavering grace. Can you accomplish some valuable projects for the district or school? Can your work garner acclaim from high-leverage stakeholders, such as the union or the school board? Can you draw continual attention to what your team has achieved through social media, school newsletters, or other public forums? Garnering a glowing reputation can help protect you from the whims of an unpredictable, tyrannical boss, who will be less prone to fire you if you have earned the love of other school denizens.

Even after building sound political credit and trying to manage up, you might find yourself feeling so trapped and hopeless that you fear you need to get out. The litmus test is simple: Do you like who you are while you're at work? Do you feel proud of the things you say and do, or do they make you feel slimy? Do you feel a cognitive disconnect between your work persona and your genuine self? If you have come to despise the person you are in the office, it's probably time to go. It's a rough decision, particularly if you've invested years of your life in your current district, but you know in your heart that you can't live a lie. You owe it to yourself to find a job in which you can be the best version of you.

In Summary

Sitting through a boss's fury fest can inflame a host of unsettling feelings. We might doubt our abilities as a leader, suspect our colleagues of slander, or else stew in frustration at our boss's volatility. As if these weren't enough, we then have to walk away pretending nothing happened, accepting the occasional temper tantrum as an inevitable part of administrator life. In these emotionally tense moments, your natural inclination might be to fight back or break down completely. Hold back those instincts and use strategies to defuse the situation, deepen your understanding of your boss's perspective, and minimize future outbursts. **Express as much agreement as you can**, building solidarity with your boss. **Ask yourself why a reasonable person would act like this** so that you can add empathy to that solidarity. **Prioritize fixing the problem**, whether or not you believe the accusations valid, and learn to **manage up**, thus reducing your chances of repeat confrontations. These techniques are challenging to master. They involve reining in your emotions and instincts, contrary to human nature. But once you master them, you will find yourself more than prepared to rise to the challenge the next time an irate supervisor wants to make you a punching bag.

4

The Struggling Salesperson

Oh, no, Katie thinks as she watches the curriculum director's presentation. *Please, no. Please don't make me do this.* It's the summer meeting, and the director has just announced that all schools will adopt standards-based grading practices this August. Homework, participation, and behavior can no longer be factored into student grades, which will reflect mastery of state standards and nothing else. All principals must implement standards-based grading in their schools immediately.

    Katie had been eager to start her fifth year as a middle school principal, but now she's filled with dread. It's not like she doesn't understand the philosophy; the director cited some compelling research during his three-hour presentation, and she knows that every other district in the area is doing standards-based grading. Still, she's not sure this will actually improve student learning. In her time as a middle school teacher, she had some very productive conversations with parents and students about the relationship between homework and learning. As a principal, she's spent the last four years painstakingly building consistent, fair expectations around study habits in her building, and she's hesitant to dismantle the system because of one sweeping edict from central office. However, this is the direction the district is going. It was even intimated that anyone who does not believe in standards-based grading is unfit for employment in the district, so voicing her concern to the higher-ups isn't exactly an option. Katie is going to have to do her part to support this initiative or risk her job.

As the school year begins, she implements standards-based grading thoroughly and faithfully. She follows the district's protocols to the letter and provides professional development on assessment practices for her staff. She explains the way grades are now calculated to students and parents with a smile on her face, conducting several parent sessions and posting explanatory videos on the school website. Still, she knows her staff hate the new practice. They're not outright rebelling—she's been their principal for long enough to earn their trust—but she can feel their scorching anger in every hallway conversation, every department meeting, and every class visit. In meetings, they ask her pointed questions: "Why don't you care whether our students participate in class?" "Don't you want to prepare kids for the real world, where there are actual consequences for not doing work?" In private, teachers break down, sharing their feelings of helplessness and frustration. She even had a teacher cry once, discouraged at her students' refusal to do homework now that it no longer counts for a grade. Every time this happens, Katie desperately wants to say, "It wasn't me! I didn't inflict this on you! I don't even agree with it!" . . . but she knows she can't. Every time the subject arises, she feels like a charlatan, parroting the lines provided by the district while wishing she could be more truthful. She wonders if there is something wrong with her. After all, plenty of the other principals love standards-based grading, and district leadership clearly researched the practice. Shouldn't she be able to put her reservations aside and just support this system?

Debrief the Doubts

We've all been in Katie's shoes. Some of us have even been in the district director's loafers, which are no more comfortable. We all receive top-down edicts, and there are struggling salespeople at every level, from first-year assistant principals dealing with district directives right on up to superintendents facing state mandates. Being handed down a program, practice, or policy and told to "make it happen" is part of our job as administrators, yet it can instantly evaporate our confidence.

I'm guessing, for instance, that you spent your first year in administration bouncing back and forth between teachers and your boss, trying to memorize the right answers to thorny questions about some policy that was in place before you were hired. I'll bet it wasn't long afterward that your district rolled out a massive program change and saddled you with the task of selling it to your teachers. Even now, you probably find yourself dreading that summer administrator meeting, waiting to learn what policy will roll down the mountain and trample your relationships with your team.

The doubt associated with marketing a proposal you didn't put forth has deep, sprawling roots, the most pernicious of which is the feeling that you are a liar. In some cases, you feel like a liar because you are, in fact, lying. You may see some benefits to the directive, but you're not totally convinced by it. Yet you must pretend to be to earn your paycheck. That's an awful feeling, one that makes you question your integrity. In other cases, you may not mind the directive, but you're not able to share all the information you'd like to. Imagine what would happen if you said certain truths aloud. For example:

- "We're doing this because our superintendent wants to keep the board president happy."
- "I fired her because my boss threatened to fire me if I didn't."
- "Everybody has to do the sexual harassment training again because Jim can't seem to text Tina without taking his pants off."

No matter how necessary, withholding information can feel just as dishonest as outright lying, and it comes with a demeaning sensation of being a marionette in a masquerade. *Is this why I got into leadership?* you ask yourself. *So I can be someone else's puppet, saying what I'm told to and unable to reveal the full truth?*

Just as gallingly, you may not even know all the reasons behind the decision to implement whatever program, practice, or policy was handed to you. The person in charge might be concealing the whole picture or might simply not have explained it very well. Whether or not you agree with the directive, you're still the one tasked with selling it to your staff. You may even find yourself tempted to improvise answers to the tricky questions they raise.

It's not just tricky questions—teachers' responses overall can erode your confidence faster than anything. Teachers do not appreciate the constant parade of changes foisted upon them, as you know if you've been in education longer than a minute. When selling a mandated change in practice, therefore, you can expect intense questioning at best—and gladiatorial combat at worst. Even when you approve of the change and are excited to see it realized, it's hard to face down an avalanche of frustration, antagonism, and downright fury with implacable grace. Staff point out flaws in the plan, express anger and resistance, and blame you for your role in all of it. These contentious interactions inflame your doubt astronomically. So what do you do when you are forced to sell something that you didn't create and maybe don't even believe in?

Avoid the Pitfalls

Don't Say, "The District Is Making Us Do This"

It's tempting, I know, to pawn off the responsibility. Trust me, those words are on the tip of my tongue every time I'm sitting in front of a teacher explaining an onerous directive that came from on high. I know how desperately you want to connect with your people by saying that, like them, you think this is stupid. I know you want them to see you as one of the good guys.

But don't do it.

Here's the thing: Teachers might know perfectly well that you are just the messenger, whether or not you say it aloud, but it doesn't mean they will cut you any slack. Why should they? You're still enforcing something they don't like. If you punt responsibility over to someone else, you're making yourself look like a crony who's sold out, and they will cut you even less slack. They'll also start to wonder whether you have any real authority, given that you look like a stooge in a despotic regime. This will hurt you in the long run. You want your teachers to see you as an authority figure when it comes time to provide instructional feedback, deliver professional development, or address improper behavior. If you ruin your credibility by sniveling about how you were forced to enact someone else's decision, you won't be able to enforce your own decisions in the future.

One final note: You *are* the district, my friend. Not because you're an administrator but because you, along with your teachers, nurses, custodians, psychologists, counselors, technicians, bus drivers, and more, make up that cornerstone of your community: the school district. Whatever your current rung on the ladder, you're not disconnected from everyone else, and your team is not an island under fire. Describing "the district" as separate from yourself denies this reality.

Don't Invent a Rationale

Yes, it's infuriating to get a directive without context (or worse, with a terrible rationale), and it's horrible to have to pass a baseless mandate along, knowing that you are compounding the sin. You may instinctively want to provide some sort of context or reasoning to your staff to show them respect. Inventing rationales for a directive, however, will make your situation immeasurably worse.

When you make up a rationale for someone else's decision, you compromise not only yourself but also every leader in the district. It's easy to see why: If you and four other building principals all invent different explanations, teachers will be confused and frustrated when they talk to each other and inevitably discover the disconnect. They'll see that the admin team doesn't take time to calibrate answers, and they'll lose whatever confidence they may have had in the program.

If you need a more personal incentive not to improvise, consider this: If your invented rationale turns out to be wrong, your reputation will be at risk when those in power find out. Sowing confusion will cause problems for the whole leadership team, and whoever has to clean up the mess will remember it.

Remember, it's better to say nothing than to spread falsehoods.

Don't Make Promises You Can't Keep

"We'd *never* get rid of our grading platform."

"I swear, parents are going to appreciate this."

"I promise, this is the last time we're changing the schedule this year."

As a struggling salesperson, you often feel powerless. That's why it's natural to grasp at whatever power you do have to try to make people happy. You want to offer them something that will calm their fears or assuage their anger.

I hate to break it to you, but you don't have as much power as you'd like. For instance, you don't have the power to see the future. You don't have the power to control other people's responses to initiatives. You don't have the power to prevent random circumstances from sabotaging your plans. You shouldn't pretend that you do. Making promises and having to break them will compound how foolish you look in exchange for the dubious short-term benefit of appeasing teachers. What's more, using shaky promises as a bargaining chip can cause just as much trouble with the higher-ups as inventing a rationale.

Navigate a Path
Put the Change in Perspective

Even if you don't initially support whatever program, practice, or policy your higher-ups have handed down, you'll eventually want to consider whether you can come around to the idea. After all, leading change is so much easier if you can embrace what you're selling. But changing your heart and mind takes time, effort, and serious reflection, so start by putting the situation into perspective. The proper perspective will help you make an informed decision whether to embrace the change when the time comes.

It's easy to understand the perspective of resisters—after all, they're standing right outside your door, voicing their agony in graphic detail. You get their perspective in the hallway, in your voicemail, and in your inbox. But there are other angles you can use to approach the issue. For example:

- **The executive perspective**—Why is the school, district, or state rolling out this change? What's the big-picture reason? If you seek to understand the rationale and it's not immoral or unethical, perhaps it can inspire you to begin to support the new system.
- **The wide-angle perspective**—How earth-shattering is this issue, really? Will it truly dismantle education in your school, leaving a war-torn wasteland, as its detractors say it will? Or is it just a temporary inconvenience while everyone adjusts? People find reasons to resist even the tiniest changes (I once witnessed actual tears when a school switched from chalkboards to whiteboards), but you don't have to buy into the frenzy. Looking through a wide-angle lens will help you assess how monumental any changes actually are and talk people around to rationality.
- **The beneficiary perspective**—Will parents, teachers, and, most of all, students benefit from this change? Maybe you're requiring staff to do something different, but if you can see the clear advantage to others, hold that image in your mind. Examine the concrete, tangible benefits over and over and let the vision guide you through the short-term pain of resistance.

Looking at the issue of standard-based grading from the executive perspective, Katie accepts the district's stated reason for the change: to ensure that grades reflect students' mastery of skills rather than their completion of tasks. *OK,* she thinks. *That's logical. That's not immoral or unethical. I can get behind it.* Then she examines it through the wide-angle perspective, imagining what her school will look like in five years. *You know what?* she realizes. *Standards-based grading will be second nature to everyone by then. People railed against the block schedule, too, but they got over it after the first year.* Finally, she looks at the benefit to students and parents, who will now know exactly what every grade means. *Just think,* she tells herself, *I won't have to explain why Mrs. Casten counts homework for 50 percent of the grade but Mr. Goodman only counts it for 10 percent! I won't need to tell students that "effort" and "participation" are different in every teacher's classroom.* Thinking through these perspectives helps Katie set herself up to embrace standards-based grading, despite her initial struggle.

It looks so easy when Katie does it, but in real life, it's tough. We've been trained to trust our gut, and if our gut reaction is opposition to a change—however trivial—we tend to plant our flag on the hill of resistance. We blow the situation up in our mind, imagining ourselves fighting injustice at every turn ("You can pry my chalkboard from my cold, dead hands!"). The trouble is that your gut can deceive you. It can tell you you're right when you're not. It can distort the importance of situations. It can make you believe that yours is the only opinion that matters. You, yourself, might be subject to the same knee-jerk aversion to change that you so often deplore in your staff. When they resist change, you cast them as obstinate and shortsighted; when you resist change, you're being ethical and righteous.

That's not a criticism. It's human nature. Knowing this, you can bring humility to your work by considering the possibility that you might, eventually, grow to embrace this change. Reflective leaders temper their gut reaction with perspective. They consider the bigger picture—the fact that education is an ecosystem with millions of stakeholders blending policy, economics, social welfare, children's well-being, and so much more. Nothing is simple or clear-cut, and there is very little on which educators unanimously agree. True reflection means knowing that your gut isn't the only one in the room, and more important, that it might not be as unwavering as you think. As you listen to proponents of a change, and as you see how the change itself plays out, you might conclude that your initial reaction was simply an impulse born of your own biases, habits, and presuppositions. We'll talk about inviolable moral lines later in the chapter, but for now, consider the issue from many perspectives as you attempt to reflect and evolve.

Be Receptive, Not Reactive

Assume your staff will have plenty of questions, at least during the initial rollout of a new program, practice, or policy. Listen to their questions, write them down, and show an eager desire to answer them. But don't respond to them until you're ready. You are *not* ready if you feel flustered, confused, or attacked; those feelings are the devils on your shoulder whispering dangerous advice such as "Tell them you're a victim, just like them!" or "You're great at improv. Just make something up!"

You are also not ready if you don't yet have the information to provide a factual answer. This seems obvious, but we sometimes picture ourselves as vending machines, obligated to crank out whatever is demanded of us; when we can't produce immediate and correct answers, we make something up so no one will lash out at us in frustration. But the expectation that you know all the answers exists only in your head. Most of your staff will not mind if you respond, "I don't know yet, but I'll find out"—especially if you do it calmly and amiably.

"Calm" and "amiable" may feel like a reach, especially if you've ever stood in front of your building staff explaining why, for example, their plan periods were cut. I'm well-acquainted with the cold sweat, dry mouth, and racing heart that ride in on the waves of a turbulent meeting. I'm also deeply familiar with the slog of long-winded emails and interminable phone calls that accompany a contested change in practice. I've made all the mistakes listed in this chapter and even a few bonus ones: losing my temper, dignifying unworthy questions, and tolerating abusive behavior, for a start.

That's how I learned that projecting a receptive, agreeable demeanor is both the simplest and most effective thing you can do when forced to sell an idea you didn't conceive. You want to show teachers how open you are to discussion and how you want to partner with them to get to a point of mutual understanding. Be aware, though, that being open to discussion isn't the same thing as being able to negotiate. It's possible—even probable—that the program, practice, or policy you're presenting is set in stone, but your staff needs to know that they can come to you with thoughts, feedback, questions, ideas, or insights. Even if you can't change the edict, you can hear them out. You can be calm and welcoming. And you can thank them for trusting you with their true perspective.

The best part? You can do all this without answering a single question before you're ready. That's why there's no need to panic when your staff starts querying or showing resistance to something you're forced to support. Instead, be ready with collaborative language such as the following:

- "That's a great point, Mario, and I really appreciate your bringing it up. I don't want to give you a hasty answer, so will you give me time to think it through?"

- "I know this new practice seems like a burden right now, but I've learned that these things feel easier and easier once you have a chance to get used to them and solve some of the early problems. For now, let's focus on thinking of solutions that could make all our lives easier."
- "I feel really lucky that you trust me with your honest opinions. I'd always rather get the truth to my face, even if it's hard to hear, than a bunch of gossip behind my back. Thank you for being sincere with me. I want you to know that I'm going to be equally truthful with you, especially about what I can or can't do and can or can't share."

Notice how these responses indicate that you don't know everything, can't change everything, and can't disclose everything, but they don't make you sound like a helpless puppet. They also signal your willingness to listen and respond when you can be truthful.

Let's think through what Katie might do and say as she converts her building's grading system. She'll want to be truthful about her own level of expertise while also committing to learning, so she might say, "To be honest, standards-based grading feels new to me, too. Like you all, I used the old-fashioned effort system when I taught. But you know what? Our school is innovative, and we want our grades to really reflect what a student knows. That's why I'm going to work with you to understand these new standard-based rubrics and calibrate our grading so that we can feel confident when report cards go out." Katie will not know every answer, but she never said she did. She may not start off as an expert, but she is committing to becoming one and she expects her staff to do the same.

Being receptive, not reactive, will enable you to maintain your relationships while you think about what to do next.

Calibrate and Construct

Following the advice above will buy you time to get more information while your people cool off and actually try whatever new program or practice you're selling. Use this time well. Make a list of the most frequently asked questions, commonly identified problems, and hotly voiced complaints, then buckle up for a long journey.

"Getting more information" sounds simple, but it can be maddeningly complex and tedious. If you ask five different colleagues the same question, you could get five different answers, even if all five people are higher on the ladder than you. Other administrators may have caved to the temptation to invent answers, fomenting the general confusion. On top of that, there may be serious problems that can't be solved by a mere phone call, making it hard, even impossible, to mollify your team.

That's why, if you're serious about getting answers, finding solutions, and addressing complaints, you're going to have to think strategically:

- **Approach people strategically.** Find the highest-ranked person willing to give you a minute of their time, and approach them first for answers, decisions, and solutions. Seek out the other salespeople struggling to uphold the party line and make it a point to include them in the conversation so you can calibrate your answers. This will help you all feel confident that you're sending the right message, and not just whatever you heard on the grapevine.
- **Select issues strategically.** Use discernment to distinguish between legitimate issues and frivolous ones. Don't convey baseless, passive-aggressive questions or complaints up the ladder; this will annoy your supervisor, and you will appear to have poor judgment. Knowing that your phrasing, attitude, and discernment are all on display, pick the most

serious issues to tackle and get the answers you need. Say, for example, that Katie needs to ask more questions about standards-based grading. Which of the following inquiries would her boss appreciate and respond to?

— "Hey boss, my department is feeling really down about this whole system. There's a lot of chatter that all our students are going to fail, especially when effort and participation won't buffer their grades. They also feel really nervous about learning the new online gradebook. Plus, they say that this whole thing doesn't prepare kids for the real world, where effort and work completion actually count. What should I do?"

— "Hey boss, I want to make sure I'm explaining our perspective on homework properly. My understanding is that homework is practice, and we don't want to penalize a kid for messing up on practice. That's why we don't grade homework, right? We only enter the summative grade because the summative is what all the practice was for. I understand the theory, but now I'm wondering how I can help teachers motivate students to actually do homework so they get the necessary practice. Will you talk me through it?"

Figure 4.1 offers some guidelines on identifying the differences between legitimate and frivolous issues.

- **Describe your predicament strategically.** No one should doubt your willingness to do your part to uphold this program, practice, or policy. Your tone of voice, body language, and phrasing should all indicate that your main goal is to implement the new system faithfully. Relaying issues up the ladder or asking peers for advice is your tactic to make sure you've got the information you need to serve the organization well.

Figure 4.1. Legitimate or Frivolous?

Legitimate Issues	Frivolous Issues
• Bound to come up ("How should we motivate kids to do their homework if it doesn't count toward their grade?")	• Highly unlikely ("What happens if every student fails every subject because this new system makes it impossible for them to pass?")
• Relevant to large groups ("Will the new digital gradebook automatically do mastery-based calculations?")	• Relevant only to tiny groups ("I have one student who missed half of last year because he was hospitalized, but his mom wants him in my class, even though Mr. Smith would be better with his reading intervention . . .")
• Heavy in impact ("How should we intervene when students are falling behind in core subjects?")	• Low in impact ("I'm nervous about learning a new way to calculate grades.")

You'll also have to be a bit pushy. You might need to organize group meetings, follow up on unanswered emails, and keep asking until you get answers. You'll feel like a pest, but it will be worth it if you can prove to your team that you can be trusted to provide them with resolution and consistency. If you wait for key information to trickle down to you, you could be stuck in a holding pattern for months while your staff grows angrier and more resistant.

Before you stop pushing for answers, think of the most challenging staff member you have. You know the one I'm talking about. Their hand is the first one in the air at meetings. Their colleagues fall silent when they speak. Their mere presence in your office makes you clench up. Put yourself in their shoes and ask,

What would that person say if they were here right now, listening to the explanation I'm getting from my boss? Would they ask more questions? Would they have more concerns? If the answer is "yes," keep poking and prying until you feel confident defending the program to that staff member—which, of course, is exactly what you'll need to do.

Katie, for instance, should probably spend extra time talking to the teachers most opposed to standards-based grading—not to pacify them but to study their concerns. She should have a deep enough grasp of what's bothering them to see the issue with their eyes; this will entail listening empathetically without breaking the party line. If she can thread that needle, she will get a sense of how to respond if the higher-ups try to brush her off or dismiss staff concerns as irrelevant.

Once you have the answers you need, practice relaying them in your own words until you sound authentic, not robotic. What's tricky here is that you may *still* not agree 100 percent with the program, practice, or policy—in truth, getting more information isn't the same thing as buying in. That's why it's important to practice your sales pitch. You can't show up to your staff meeting with a list of answers to questions, only to read them off in a begrudging monotone. Think how your skepticism will infect your team and make your own predicament worse. Construct a platform from which you can confidently answer questions and work through problems as you uphold the new system.

Part and Personalize

If you don't *have* to gather your people together in a group to watch you defend a hated change, don't—at least not right away. We'll explore the hazards of these meetings in the mob mollifier chapter, but for now, think about how much easier it is to have a casual, one-on-one conversation with a colleague, even if they disagree with everything you say, than to stand in front of a mutinous horde. You'll get better results from 15 one-hour conversations with individuals than a one-hour conversation with a 15-person mob. The mob will likely treat you as a tool of the establishment, but the individuals will likely treat you as a human. The mob will try to trip you up, but the individual will hear you out. The mob will claim you're not listening, but the individual gets your undivided attention.

Find ways of talking separately with as many people as possible, matching the method to the person. Some might appreciate formal meetings in your office if they have a lot to say, but others will see this as intimidating and would prefer a quick hallway chat. Your overall goal with each individual meeting isn't necessarily to convert hearts and minds, it's to gain the following information:

- **Insight into each person's outlook and morale.** Making your staff feel heard and valued is the best way to maintain relationships while still upholding the change that was handed down to you.
- **A sense of what's *really* causing resistance.** Do people not like the program because they don't think it will work? Do they not like the practice because it's more paperwork for them? Do they not like the policy because they weren't involved in its creation? Getting an idea of the root causes of resistance will help you respond appropriately to each person.
- **A clear picture of how widespread the opposition to the new program, practice, or policy is.** What you learn might surprise you. People who support change are often quiet in big meetings, letting naysayers run the show. You

may find out that some of your quieter team members like the new system. As you talk with more and more people, you'll be able to gauge whether *everyone* opposes the change or just a few noisy naysayers.

Tailor your tone and words to the person sitting in front of you. Some people just want you to listen, meaning all you have to do is empathize. Others will want answers to their questions. Still others might like coaching or guidance. By differentiating for each person, you can meet their needs while also satisfying your desire to give people what they want.

Let's look at Katie's situation. She knows her staff well, having been their principal for several years, so she makes a point to connect individually with each person in a way they'll find valuable, and she uses each conversation to gain insight. She notices that the teachers who are opposed to standards-based grading mainly fear what will happen if students ignore homework and class activities. These teachers have spent so much time developing their lesson plans that it hurts to see students ignore an activity when it doesn't count for a grade. Katie now realizes she is dealing with fear, not hostility. She feels more empathy for the people she'd previously labeled as opponents, and she dedicates herself to helping these teachers engage students. Other staff actually love the change, but they are reluctant to go against what they perceive to be popular opinion. Katie finds ways to build their confidence, eventually empowering them to speak on behalf of the grading system.

Decide Whether You Can Embrace the Change

Where possible, convince your own heart and mind to support the practice, program, or policy. If you're advocating for something you believe in, you'll feel less like an impostor when you stand in front of your staff and uphold the change. You might still need to polish your phrasing or calibrate your answers, but your doubts will evaporate. What's more, you will lead through this change more effectively than if you remain a beleaguered, conflicted salesperson. I ask you to consider embracing the change for the sake of your sanity and efficacy.

This might take a while. You may need to see the effects of the change in action or engage in thoughtful conversations with other leaders before you can really embrace it. That's perfectly OK. If we all dug our heels in and stuck with our immediate reaction to change, no one would ever make progress, but leaders are reflective people. We can conquer our initial reactions and reservations. We can see through multiple perspectives and discern serious issues from frivolous ones. In doing so, you may slowly come to embrace the new program, practice, or policy, however unpleasant it initially seemed.

Truly embracing the change is the hardest part of our navigation, and honestly, it may not be possible in every circumstance. There are some changes you simply won't be able to embrace, some policies that grate against your conscience. A mandate might be morally or ethically troubling to you. Things get personal here. You must decide for yourself: Can you *enforce* the change even if you don't *embrace* it? If you can, make sure to arm yourself with some of the strategies outlined here so that you can maintain your relationships with staff and present a united front with other leaders. It will be hard, but know that you're not alone; plenty of leaders find a way to enforce practices they personally disagree with.

If you cannot enforce the change due to moral or ethical conflicts, you have yet another decision to make: Are you willing to try speaking up to the people with power to explain your opposition? What, exactly, do you hope to get out of that conversation? What are you willing to risk if the conversation goes sideways or if your defiance angers the higher-ups?

Let's assume that you are willing to speak up, no matter the cost. I suggest going to your immediate supervisor first. It's true that they may not have any more power to change the program, practice, or policy than you do, but at least you can communicate to them how deeply this issue troubles you and get a sense of where they stand. You may also get an ally in your quest to challenge the system. Then, bring your concerns as high up the ladder as you feel comfortable.

This might mean getting involved in state or local politics. Since you can't flout actual laws, no matter how much you disagree with them, you might need to go straight to the source: lawmakers. Ironically, it can be easiest to push back against state mandates; think how much easier it is to fire off an email to a state senator than to tell your superintendent you disagree with their policy. You can get involved with lobbying groups and professional organizations, reach out directly to your elected representatives, or register comments during public meetings. As a professional educator, you have a right—even a duty—to make your voice heard as educational policy is created.

No matter who you're talking to, though, bring the facts. Do you have any evidence that this program is actively harming students or staff? Do you have metrics showing how widespread the damage is? Do you have firsthand accounts from victims? You *must* go into these conversations with hard facts, or else you will appear hysterical, insubordinate, or incompetent. You also have to be clear about what response you want, whether a change in policy or simply an acknowledgment of the concerns.

Finally, think before you act. This issue might be worth losing or vacating your job, but make that decision with a cool head and a full set of facts. Before doing anything rash, ask yourself whether you can find ways of adapting your practices even within the confines of policies that chafe your conscience. Maybe you can meet the requirements demanded of you but add your own flair. Can you prioritize, accommodate, or arrange your work in a way that allows you to obey the rules while also feeling good about it?

Fortunately, most top-down edicts are not moral crucibles awaiting the sacrifice of righteous martyrs. Most struggling salespeople are simply caught between the people above and below them, trying to liaise with dignity. This is a challenging but manageable position and one made more comfortable by at least trying to embrace the change.

In Summary

Selling someone else's program, practice, or policy can shake the confidence of even the most veteran leaders. We feel like pawns, reciting the rote lines provided to us from on high, struggling to keep up the pretense through every contentious conversation with staff. This nagging doubt can make a leader feel weak, but know this: You're not weak unless you give into your base temptations. If you pass blame by saying, "The district is making us do this," invent a rationale, or make promises you can't keep, that's weakness. If, however, you dig into your sales briefcase and deploy some useful tools, you're showing strength and skill. Start by **putting the change into perspective**, looking at it from a variety of angles and considering possibilities. **Be receptive, not reactive**, by listening more than you talk—at least at first. Then,

calibrate and construct answers to the most common questions with other leaders in your district. **Part and personalize** your interactions with staff, thus enabling you to get a sense of what's really going on. Finally, try to **embrace the change**, which will make your sales pitch more sincere and your doubts less consequential.

5

The Mob Mollifier

Elena is on a roll. Months of research, planning, and stakeholder meetings have brought her to this: a pivotal presentation to district staff explaining the new student discipline policy, which she has long championed as an equitable shift. She's absolutely crushed the slideshow, and she can't wait to start the open discussion. As a newly hired assistant superintendent, Elena is ready to bask in the support for her exciting initiative.

A hand hits the air.

"So, basically, you're telling us there are no more consequences for misbehavior?" a teacher asks, visibly shaking with rage. Around her, other staff nod and mutter, and more hands go up. "Which teachers did you cherry-pick for your little committee?" another teacher asks, while a social worker jumps in with, "You're treating our schools like pawns to make yourself look better!" To Elena's horror, an assistant principal stands up. "Just so you know, the building admins all think this is garbage," he says. "It's going to totally disrupt our school environments."

Elena feels a mix of confusion and panic. *What is happening right now?* she wonders. *We had teacher committees and polls.*

We collaborated with union leadership. We did school board presentations, for goodness' sake! How is this breaking down after all our careful planning?

She manages to get everyone's attention and hurriedly points out that the district did, in fact, consult every stakeholder group. As she clicks back to the slides showing the many committees involved in the decision-making process, the noise level rises again. Teachers shout that they didn't see the opinion poll, that there should have been more communication about the proposed change, that district representatives should have gone door to door collecting teacher perspectives. To hear them tell it, the district maliciously deceived every employee, and their professional efficacy is being sacrificed on an altar of politics.

Elena is getting angry. It seems to her like these people ignored the proposed change while it was still hypothetical, but now that it's happening, they suddenly want to get involved. They've probably been stirred up by some social media group they all treat as gospel. They also don't seem to understand the bigger picture, the real reasons why this policy is so important, or the benefits it will have for the whole community. She wants very much to respond with indignant explanations that this decision was reached through the proper methods, that their elected union representatives approved it, and that they can take their hysterical whining to someone who cares.

Of course, she can't. Elena has to stand there and defend the new policy against the mob. What's more, she has to do it without saying or doing anything to jeopardize her own position. She cannot lose her temper, disclaim responsibility for the change, or even reprove the teachers' rowdy behavior. Acting defensive or belligerent will make her appear weak, as will breaking down and apologizing meekly when she knows there is nothing to apologize for. On the other hand, the more she allows the group to throw around false accusations and work themselves into a frenzy, the harder it will be to keep her cool and bring things to a clear resolution.

As her heart pounds and her blood runs cold, Elena knows her job—and perhaps her career—will be affected by what she does next. Her predecessor found himself in hot water after losing the good opinion of the teaching staff, the consequence of several tense meetings like this one. If, like him, Elena gains a reputation for being domineering, callous, and unresponsive to teachers' concerns, she's in for a world of trouble.

Debrief the Doubts

If I could command leadership programs to add one outcome to their curriculum, it would be this: *Learn to manage an angry mob without damaging your relationships, your reputation, or your efficacy.* The fact that most graduate programs gloss over this topic when every single administrator will, at some point, come up against an irate throng is downright neglectful.

Sometimes, you walk into the room knowing you're about to face a combative mob. Maybe you're holding the party line on a despised policy or delivering news that you know is unpopular. If you're a struggling salesperson, you're also defending someone else's decision, meaning you may lack the genuine passion that helps many leaders face down mass opposition.

Nothing is as horrible, however, as being caught off guard. The specter of a mob is especially terrifying because it can break out anytime, anywhere, with no rhyme or reason. You can be having a perfectly normal meeting about one topic, only to have attendees bring up another topic out of nowhere; they all pile on, and suddenly, you're facing a mob. You quickly disprove the graduate school mythology that, if you simply execute the proper steps, people will cheerfully follow along with your leadership. In fact, you can do everything right—like Elena, you can plan collaboratively, seek stakeholder feedback, communicate a clear outline—and *still* find yourself under attack. It's galling to watch a defiant crowd erupt when you've been so diligent and conscientious. You thought you'd covered every base, anticipated every concern, and factored in every perspective, yet here you are, confronted with torches and pitchforks.

The stakes are high. Dozens, maybe hundreds, of people are watching as you make split-second decisions under immense pressure. They will repeat what you say and do, sharing your failures far and wide. Some of them will distort what you actually say and do based on their overall impression. I've listened in confusion as people described a leader "screaming" or "crying" during a meeting that I attended where I saw no such thing. All it takes is one word in the wrong ear for your reputation to suffer.

In that crucial moment, as you're being pelted with barbed questions and challenged ruthlessly, your body may mutiny as well. Your hands shake and your voice trembles. Your blood turns to ice and your head fills with buzzing. Your heart pounds so violently that you swear people can see your chest thumping. Worst of all, your basest instincts storm to the front lines of your brain. Those instincts might be vicious, prompting you to threaten, mock, and snap back in the same hostile tone as your attackers. Or your instincts might be meeker, though equally harmful: you might be inclined to cajole, bargain, backpedal, or break down and cry.

You know, intellectually, that you should be capable of wrangling the mob back into line, but it sounds impossible in the face of people you've known for years showing just how nasty and spiteful they can be. Previous encounters with angry mobs, which no one prepared you for, may have seen you giving into damaging impulses, leaving you with regrets and painful memories but no more preparation for the next showdown.

Doubt bubbles up as you wonder whether you allowed this mob to arise through some fault of your own. Maybe you mismanaged something and are reaping what you've sown. You also doubt whether there is any way to end this meeting without damaging relationships or your reputation—not to mention whatever plan you're discussing. You're in a room with dozens of outraged people, your own emotions are spiraling out of control, and your future in the district is on the line. So how do you get an angry mob under control without resorting to threats or backpedaling?

Avoid the Pitfalls
Don't Clap Back

When we're under attack, we want to defend ourselves. It's instinctive. It's also a great way to get yourself in trouble.

You so desperately want to clap back, to let your snarky retorts or angry explanations flow freely, especially when you know you're justified and the mob's criticisms are unfounded. It's even more enticing when your audience members are wildly out of line, behaving deplorably because they have you cornered. They know you have to smile placidly throughout their tantrums, so they flaunt their freedom to act out. This tempts you to get on your high horse and put the hooligans in their place.

Unfortunately, such a response will prompt an endless back-and-forth exchange, and even your best defenses will appear, well, defensive. You'll look petty at best and volatile at worst. Here's why: Your emotions, rather than your intellect, fuel those instinctive responses. The entire room will see your composure dissolve into panic, anger, fear, sarcasm, belligerence, or confusion. These are not the emotions people admire in their leaders. You'll damage your reputation, sparking endless rumors about how you "lost it" during the meeting. When you try to regain your team's respect, they'll remember your snide remarks or frantic justifications, and they'll think about how you sank to the level of the naysayers, nitpickers, and ne'er-do-wells.

Remember this: The mob may disperse, but the members of the mob will be in your life for years to come. You're going to have to interact with them again and again. The worst thing you can do is damage relationships and your reputation by saying something careless, spiteful, or belligerent in front of the whole group.

Don't Bargain

Faced with everything from quibbling to staunch opposition, you might be tempted to negotiate, wheedle, or backpedal: "Let's just do half of these things for next year." "Please try it—you might like it." "OK, we'll return to the drawing board and present another plan."

If you're the intermediary, you might also tell them that you'll "go back and see" if the plan or policy can be changed based on feedback. You try to validate everyone's criticisms and concerns, and you adjust your directives.

Bargaining with the mob might feel virtuous initially; after all, good leaders listen to their team's concerns and respond accordingly. But let's be honest: If your response is prompted by mob action, you're not *responding accordingly* so much as *placating desperately*. You're trying to pacify people to get yourself out of an uncomfortable situation.

Insidiously, bargaining validates unworthy, irrelevant, or self-serving criticism. Take Elena's situation. Her detractors complain that they were not given sufficient opportunities for input, but this is demonstrably untrue. She sent out polls, created teacher committees, and collaborated with union leadership. Elena can disregard this criticism with a clear conscience. The mob will say she could have done more, which is of course true; leaders can always do more. What we strive to do, however, is *enough*—and if we've done enough to proceed with integrity, we don't need to feel guilty or resort to bargaining. Elena doesn't have to grovel and apologize for not meeting individually with every employee to gain their personal blessing on the new plan.

Moreover, if you bargain, you teach people that mob action gets results, that when they don't like what you're saying, they should attack and you will recant. Don't set that precedent. Don't reward unprofessional behavior with obsequious pleas for approval. Keep in mind how much worse it will be for yourself and your team if you go down the treacherous path of bargaining and backpedaling.

Don't Feel Compelled to Answer Everything Immediately

Members of the mob love to ask tricky questions. They're *trying* to trap you into a corner, to make you appear foolish, tyrannical, or unprepared. They want your plan or policy to unravel, so they're going to pull at every loose thread and batter you with unworthy questions, which, as you know from Chapter 1, are manipulative, disingenuous, or unrealistic. They might also make valid inquiries that simply catch you off guard. When you inevitably get questions you aren't prepared for, your desire to appear self-assured will overpower your common sense, urging you to invent an answer to every one, no matter how tricky, trivial, unexpected, or unworthy.

If you allow manipulative, disingenuous, or unrealistic questions to dominate the meeting, the consequences will plague you for weeks or even months. Whatever plan or policy you're upholding will be hard to enforce; people will associate it with its chaotic rollout. The mob will have poisoned the well even further by planting seeds of doubt in their colleagues' minds; their "what ifs" and "yeah, buts" will buzz around the watercooler long after the meeting has ended. Then you'll struggle to rebuild trusting relationships not only with the angry participants but also with those who sat quietly through a meeting in which you let a mob run rampant. They will have seen you lose control of the room and possibly your own emotions. You'll have to rebuild your credibility slowly and painstakingly, all because you let yourself be led by the nose into trap after trap.

Refuse to answer unworthy questions point-blank. Know that indulging a manipulative, disingenuous question will harm you and your cause. When you receive valid questions you don't have an answer for, resist the urge to improvise or speculate. If you guess at an answer and turn out to be wrong, you will have to recant, which will anger people further, and you will cause trouble for your fellow leaders, who will also have to correct the misconception.

Navigate a Path
Listen More Than You Talk

You may have noticed the bait for all three traps into which mob mollifiers fall is *talking*. What you say has the potential to cause massive trouble; if retorts, bargains, or half-baked answers fly out of your mouth, you'll regret it, and you want to walk out of this meeting with zero regrets. To be clear, being regret-free is not the same as "winning." You're not going to win against a mob. Once a crowd is riled up, they're not going to listen patiently to your explanation, reconsider their attitude, and flock joyfully to your side, all in a single meeting. The very idea is ludicrous. In the moment, however, our desire to "win" tricks us into thinking it's possible.

So you're not going to win, but you want to look back on this meeting with something other than self-recrimination. Here's the key: Talk a little, listen a lot. Make a point of demonstrating your willingness to listen. The best way to do this is to respond to criticisms, concerns, and even questions with questions such as the following types:

- **Clarifying**—"Can you explain that a bit more?"
- **Probing**—"What would happen if that were the case?"
- **Funneling**—"So what's the root cause of that issue?"
- **Anything else that occurs to you**

Let's consider how Elena might respond to some of the missives lobbed at her by her angry staff:

Teacher: "So basically you're telling us there are no more consequences for misbehavior?"

Elena: "Can you explain your thinking a bit? I'd love to hear more about why the new discipline policy comes across that way."

* * *

Staff member: "You're treating our schools like pawns to make yourself look better!"

Elena: "What path would give you more agency so that you didn't feel like a pawn?"

* * *

Administrator: "Just so you know, the building admin all think this is garbage. It's going to totally disrupt our school environments."

Elena: "What makes you think a disruption is going to happen?"

The questions matter, of course, but the tone in which they're asked is even more crucial. We've all seen leaders respond to questions with questions with a smug, self-important smirk, as though they've wittily disarmed their critics. This attitude will irritate your audience and lead to a combative back-and-forth altercation, just like any snappy retort. Imagine Elena rolling her eyes and saying, "How do you *know* the disruption is going to happen? Do you have a crystal ball? Can you see into the future? We have a psychic here, ladies and gents!" Clearly, she'd lose her audience. If, however, she keeps a relaxed posture, a curious tone, and a sincere expression, she can safely say, "I'm wondering about this disruption you mentioned; what makes you think it is going to happen?"

Try to project eager interest. You want to learn more about your audience's perspective—not so you can defeat them but so you can build bridges. They're positioning themselves against you, but you're gently dissolving the idea of "sides" and gathering people around a common cause. Your nonverbal communication must give this impression, or your words will mean nothing. Even if your nerves are shredded, you have to relax your body. Take a deep breath and exhale, releasing the tension from your face and shoulders. If you can bring yourself to smile, do so. Listen to your vocal pitch—when we're under pressure, we tend to speak in a high, tight voice, often at double our normal pace, which undercuts the serene vibe you want to project. Pull your pitch back down to normal and speak deliberately and slowly.

Listening with an air of eager curiosity pays dividends. First, it maintains your reputation as a conscientious, responsive leader who parries criticisms with patient inquiries underpinned by a (hopefully) sincere desire to learn more. Asking for more information communicates a calm and receptive, rather than defensive, demeanor. Moreover, it shifts the focus to your audience members. When you invite people to explain their thinking, you subtly test the assumptions made by those asking unworthy questions or hurling unfounded accusations. You're finding a balance: You're not outright dismissing anyone's concerns, but you're not automatically assuming every criticism is valid. Best of all, this is one way to deflect questions that you can't—or shouldn't—answer.

If you do it right, this technique can also keep the temperature in the room from boiling over. Your own relaxed demeanor, your willingness to listen, and your careful management of the conversation can de-escalate some of the volatile emotions. Not all of them, of course. Your audience might still hate whatever plan you're describing, but they probably won't hate *you*. It's hard to hate a leader who eagerly listens to your perspective. They may even feel vaguely satisfied; they have vented their thoughts to a receptive listener, and may even have run out of steam when you didn't fuel their rage with snarky retorts or upsetting answers. If not, it's OK. Your primary goal is to get to the end of the meeting without saying something you will regret. Even if this is all you can do, it's still a major achievement.

Structure the Conversation

So you've mastered the art of listening more than you talk, and you can run a vitriolic meeting without saying something you'll regret. Excellent. Your next step is to structure the conversation—specifically, to manage the unworthy questions, balance the loudest voices, and lower the temperature.

Let's start with those unworthy questions. As I mentioned earlier, one way to respond to manipulative, disingenuous, or unrealistic questions is with your own questions, assuming an attitude of eager curiosity. This may prompt the crowd to qualify or scale down the query into something more rational or realistic, but not always. Some in the crowd will answer your question, then demand an answer to their own, probably with increased intensity. That's why you need additional tricks up your sleeve.

The "parking lot" is a classic tactic, and for good reason. By inviting your participants to post any and every question in a common location—a spot on the wall, a digital forum—you send the message that you welcome inquiries but cannot commit to answering them during the meeting. People will, inevitably, ignore the parking lot and sling questions at you regardless, but you can confidently redirect them and maintain the structure of your conversation. Justify the use of the parking lot by stressing your limited meeting time ("I want to make sure we cover all this material in our 30 minutes") or by assuring participants that you want to provide them with thorough answers ("I need a day or two to get you the right information"). You'll park not only unworthy questions but also legitimate questions you don't have an immediate answer for—the ones you actually do need more time to think about.

When you review the parking lot, you can choose how to answer questions. You might, for instance, create a digital Q&A list of broad topics for everyone to read, and you might answer specific questions privately with individuals. Remember, however, that you aren't required to entertain the unworthy questions on the level they're asked. Let's say someone writes, "What happens when everyone quits because they hate this discipline policy?" You do not have to entertain this absurd hypothetical. That would be sinking to the level of the manipulative questioner. You can, however, respond, "Many people expressed concerns about how sustainable this policy is. I'd like to provide an overview of our long-term plan to build teacher capacity and confidence."

Another technique for responding to unworthy questions is to call out their meritless qualities point-blank. You can choose to explain to the group that you won't be answering this question because it's manipulative, unrealistic, or disingenuous. This is challenging but doable. Again, it's all in your tone. If you sound angry, sarcastic, or patronizing, you'll inflame your audience.

For instance, responding to the question about everyone quitting with, "Did you really just ask me that? Give me a break. I'm not even going to dignify that asinine question with a response. Ask something that isn't completely unrealistic, then we'll talk" probably won't get you very far. On the other hand, picture Elena smiling calmly and compassionately as she radiates an aura of someone who understands the teacher's anger and empathizes with his fear. She says, "Kevin, I get it. There's a lot of anxiety, even animosity, toward this policy. But we're not going to start catastrophizing and coming up with solutions to very unlikely hypotheticals. It's better if we stick to the here and now and focus on how to be successful this year." This patient, empathetic response points out the unrealistic nature of the question without sounding accusatory.

This technique is powerful. It demonstrates that, far from letting unworthy questions derail the meeting, you will drain them of their power by exposing their unworthiness.

You can also structure the conversation by balancing the loudest voices in the room. Often, the same two or three people dominate the discussion, while a silent majority sits mutely by. This makes it hard to gauge how fervent the opposition actually is. Does everyone hate what you're saying, or just a noisy few? Do the silent others secretly support you, or are they ambivalent? You obviously need to bring more voices into the conversation to figure all this out, but it's tricky. There is a reason the quiet people are being quiet. Chances are, they're intimidated; they might fear being attacked if they speak up, and they're probably also concerned that they're alone in their viewpoint.

You need to make it safe for the quiet people to participate. There are entire books about building a safe culture in which team members candidly and respectfully share their mind. By all means, read those, but know that sometimes you need a quick trick. Mobs aren't always composed of carefully cultivated team members—you might present to parents, community members, or district staff outside your sphere of influence—so you don't always have the power to prevent mob action through proactive culture building. Try one or both of these techniques to bring a silent majority into the conversation on the fly:

- **Compel written participation instead of spoken participation.** Give participants a prompt ("Rank your overall satisfaction level," "List your top three emotions," "Write your most burning question") and have them write their answers anonymously either on paper or on a digital forum such as Jamboard or Padlet. You can then identify common themes, which will give you a sense of how popular the squeaky wheels' perspectives are. If you anticipate resistance, consider creating a digital poll, survey, or discussion forum ahead of time. Mentimeter, WordCloud, and their ilk are wonderful ways to solicit quick written participation; participants can use any electronic device to post their opinions or questions, and nearly all such tools allow anonymous posting. You can solicit responses either in advance or during the meeting, but make sure to draw attention to your desire to ensure that all voices are heard. The quiet ones may well feel relieved, and even the loudest critics can at least understand the rationale behind the request.

- **Break the mob up into small groups.** Assign three to five people to a group, then set them a specific task: discuss issues, summarize concerns, brainstorm solutions, or the like. This gives quiet participants a less intimidating forum to share their perspective and reduces the loud militants' influence. (If you want to be extra sneaky, you can cluster the most aggressive people into a single group, thus preventing them from bullying others.) You might ask groups to post notes from their conversation in a visible location, which will invite your aggressive critics to acknowledge a diversity of outlooks. Again, make sure to explain why you're restructuring the meeting midstream. Participants—the loudest and the quietest alike—need to hear you say how important it is to include everyone in the discussion.

These techniques increase the number of contributing voices and make it safer for quiet participants to jump in, but please note that they don't guarantee you support. It's entirely possible that the quiet people dislike your plan just as much as the trenchant ones do. The purpose of balancing the voices in the room is not to garner support but rather to accurately assess how widespread the opposition truly is. Whatever you discover, at least you will know your information comes from more than two or three squeaky wheels.

Finally, bring structure to a contentious meeting by lowering the metaphorical temperature in the room. Your goal is to cool off the heated exchanges. Again, your nonverbal communication helps: Keep your body relaxed, your tone friendly, and your expression enthusiastic. People subconsciously mirror each other's nonverbal communication, so you may find your participants maintaining this attitude, but if not, you've still set yourself up to be part of the solution rather than the problem. Try to find ways to explicitly encourage respectful discourse and redirect hostile remarks, such as "OK team, it seems like we're getting ourselves worked up here. Let's take a 10-minute break, then pick this up again with cooler heads" or "I understand emotions are running strong here, but I have to ask you not to engage in personal attacks. I know we're better than this, so let's keep it professional, please."

You can also lower the temperature by simply showing participants you care. Summarize their concerns. Reiterate their questions. Thank them for their candor. Tell them that you'd rather have them be honest, even when it's hard to hear, than snipe behind your back. Assure them that you will be in the trenches with them as they adjust to whatever new program or policy you're presenting.

Structuring the conversation is harder than simply listening more than you talk, but it has a much bigger payoff. You can generate a productive discussion, strengthen team relationships, and maybe even defuse opposition by employing techniques that keep the discourse focused and balanced.

Know When to Pull the Plug

This is where I burst your bubble. Listening eagerly and managing the conversation skillfully can keep most meetings under control, but sometimes the temperature in the room is simply too high. When the hostility reaches a fever pitch in spite of all your efforts, it's best to call the meeting off midstream. Knowing when to pull the plug is excruciatingly difficult, especially because you must decide quickly, under immense pressure, in front of an audience. In the heat of such a moment, I weigh the consequences of canceling against the consequences of continuing, and I choose whichever path minimizes my risk.

Let's apply this principle to Elena's situation. Let's say her meeting starts to go completely off the rails. She's tried her best to keep the peace, but the crowd is raging harder than ever. Professional conduct has gone out the window. Elena's request for raised hands and questions parked neatly in the lot falls on deaf ears. Participants disregard her, talking over each other and working themselves into a rampage. Each comment is louder and more hostile than the last, and most feature literal yelling and cursing. Multiple people are crying, and Elena fears she may soon be one of them. She evaluates her options.

Continuing the meeting means allowing inappropriate behavior to proliferate. She may end up pursuing disciplinary action against employees, which will cause her to look like a tyrant cutting down martyrs. What's more, the crowd might start verbally attacking each other, and if Elena allows this to happen right under her nose, she will be just as culpable as the attackers. This will damage her relationships with assailants and victims alike. On the other hand, if she tries and fails to control the room, the mob will see her as impotent. Elena herself is close to tears, so she risks displaying emotional instability. She may end up sobbing or yelling if she lets the meeting continue, which would irreparably damage her reputation.

Canceling the meeting means kicking the can down the road. The issue won't go away just because Elena pulls the plug on this meeting. At some point, she will have to find ways to reopen the conversation. She now knows one format that *doesn't* work—full staff meetings—so she can consider smaller group discussions, webinars, or even one-on-one chats to prevent another mob. Still, who knows what people will say or do between this meeting and the next? Elena also can't control how people will perceive her if she pulls the plug. They might see her as weak, incapable, or uncommitted. They might accuse her of denying them a voice in an important debate. Some of them will probably follow her down the hall after the ostensible end of the meeting, determined to make her hear them out.

Caught between two lousy options, Elena has to assess which holds the most risk. In this case, she decides that continuing the meeting is worse than canceling it. The consequences for continuing—damaged relationships, disciplinary action, volatile emotions—are dangerous and inevitable. Elena will lose her ability to lead this team. If, however, she cancels, she can mitigate the damage with skillful handling of the follow-up conversations.

Calling a meeting off midstream is a last resort. You might feel like a failure as you pull the plug. After all, you are the leader and you failed to get the mob under control. You might fear they'll lose respect for you or worry that whatever plan or policy you're upholding will fall apart now that you've let a mob dismantle your rollout. The best antidote to this dread is the clear conscience that comes from conducting yourself with dignity during the meeting and never threatening, bargaining, pleading, clapping back, or saying something you wouldn't want broadcast on the evening news. A clear conscience also comes from doing your best to manage unworthy questions, bring all voices into the discussion, and prevent the temperature from reaching a boiling point.

To pull the plug gracefully, start with an open acknowledgment of what's happening in the room. Whether people are resorting to personal attacks or emotions are running too high for rational discussion, describe what you're seeing in straightforward but respectful terms, then use it as a basis for ending the meeting. For example, you could say, "At this point, we're shouting at each other, and I value our team too much to let this continue" or "Emotions are running really high right now, and

I see people getting upset. It's not a safe environment in which to conduct such an important discussion."

Follow this statement with a promise of further action, a guarantee that you are not dismissing the mob's concerns. They will be more likely to leave the meeting peacefully if they know exactly how you plan to follow up. Given that at least one full group meeting has exploded into chaos, you might want to consider continuing the conversation in a different format: small focus groups, digital forums, or even one-on-one meetings with the most impacted individuals.

As you explain how and when you will resume the discussion, keep your tone keen and optimistic. Although you are calling it quits on this particular meeting, your subtext should say, "I hear you and I care about what you're saying, even if I don't agree. I still believe we can have a productive discussion about this, and I'm looking forward to trying again, this time in a format that works better for everyone." You want your audience to walk away believing that their leader was listening and is setting the stage for a more productive exchange in the future. If you can call the meeting to a close *and* make your audience see it as the right decision, you're setting yourself up for success as well. You will have demonstrated wisdom and discernment, which can only help you when the time comes to follow up.

In Summary

The angry mob is most administrators' worst nightmare. One minute, you're having a perfectly normal meeting; the next, your audience is in an uproar, their accusations and criticisms reaching a spiteful pitch. No one is mob-proof. Even the most experienced veterans face mobs when promoting change, upholding policies, or simply leading through difficult times. Angry hordes inflame our doubts, making us wonder whether our teams hated us all along, whether we were negligent in our planning, or whether we might not be cut out for this leadership business. It doesn't help that our brains go feral when facing a mob, tempting us to clap back, bargain, or respond brazenly to every question.

When managing a mob, the simplest guideline is to **listen more than you talk**, which prevents you from saying something you will regret and solidifies your image as a compassionate, reasonable, engaged leader. If you've mastered this technique, try **structuring the conversation** by managing unworthy questions, balancing the loudest voices, and lowering the temperature of the room. Finally, **know when to pull the plug** on the meeting by calculating the risk of continuing and deciding whether it's worth it. You will face angry mobs for the rest of your career, but you will fear them less with these tools up your sleeve.

6

The Short Straw

"Sure, I'll do it."

The words fly out of Jake's mouth automatically in response to the superintendent's request. She wants him to substitute for the kindergarten principal, who will be out for months due to a sudden illness. Put on the spot by his boss's boss, Jake knows he has to say yes.

There's just one problem: Jake has zero elementary experience. He taught high school for 10 years, then served as the district math coordinator in his first administrative job. Sure, he visits the kindergarten sometimes to observe classes and help set up math activities, but he has no idea how the building actually works. There seem to be dozens of routines built into each day—arrival, dismissal, lunch, recess—as well as a hundred processes for individual crises—lockdown procedures, disciplinary flowcharts, field trip guidelines, and so much more. It would be one thing if he'd been hired as the principal from the start of the school year, but it's February. The rules are in place, and an entire staff is expecting him to keep the ship afloat.

Jake walks nervously into the kindergarten the following morning, expecting the worst. It happens. A fight breaks out between two boys; Jake grabs the aggressor, only to hear a shout from the only other adult nearby. "Don't do that!" she bellows. "We only use de-escalation holds." *What's a de-escalation hold?* he wonders, recoiling instinctively. He tries to ask for more information, but the teacher or maybe social worker or psychologist (he hardly knows anyone) has rushed off and the secretary is calling to say that an irate parent is here to discuss the school's disciplinary policy, about which Jake knows precisely nothing. Before he reaches the office, however, a cafeteria worker dashes up and tells him the student lunch order is late, then asks him what to do. Jake is stunned to hear that the school orders student lunches every day; as math coordinator, he never knew or cared how the school cafeterias are stocked. He's about to tell them to just order pizzas (*That's the answer, right?*), but he's interrupted by a teacher leading a sobbing student toward him. To his horror, he recognizes a boy from the fight, which apparently continued the moment he turned his back. The student's arm is bleeding, and guilt overwhelms Jake, who now realizes his mistake in walking away. Half an hour on the job, and he's already responsible for an injured student.

It goes on and on. Everyone from the teachers to the custodial staff looks to Jake for skills he simply doesn't have. They want him to coax defiant students into compliance ("But I have no idea how to make him stand up and go to lunch!"). They forward phone calls to him with no context ("Wait, you're from the Department of Child and Family Services?"). They ask him to de-escalate violent students in the "calm down room" ("But I taught seniors! They don't bite this much! Am I supposed to get a shot or something?").

Jake used to think he was a decent administrator. It seems incredible that the same degree that certified him to be the math coordinator qualifies him to be a kindergarten principal, even though the two jobs couldn't be more different. Grad school was heavy on leadership theory but light on saber-toothed 5-year-olds. Why is everyone acting like he should inherently know the answer to every question simply because he's an administrator?

Maybe I'm the problem, he thinks. *Maybe I'm lacking some innate qualities of a leader, and that's why I can't seem to do anything right in this school.* Jake wonders if this is a sign that he's not cut out for leadership.

Debrief the Doubts

Whatever your role, at one time or another, you've certainly been handed some unpleasant, ill-fitting task that no one else wanted to do. Maybe you're a curriculum director who was ordered to vet classroom safety hardware. Maybe you're an elementary principal who was "voluntold" to ensure district compliance with state training mandates. Undoubtedly, you were forced to expand your horizons during the pandemic, perhaps taking on such roles as technology help associate, family resource coordinator, or vaccination pod organizer, regardless of your actual job title.

How I wish this only happened to newbies, but it continues long after your early days in a district. In fact, the more experienced and skilled you are, the more likely the higher-ups are to throw some bizarre, nettlesome task at you. Sometimes, your boss—or their boss, or their boss's boss—pretends to ask for your consent, approaching you with apparent hesitation and fawning with gratitude when you "agree" to the assignment, but you both know what's going on. You have to say yes. If you resist, you'll swiftly be reminded that your job description features the phrase "other duties as assigned," the gold standard of intentionally vague catchalls. Your boss will command you to take on the task, and you will have achieved nothing other than making yourself look lazy. The charade of asking you simply makes your boss feel better, even if it does nothing to relieve your doubts.

And those doubts hit hard. There's a reason this task has rolled downhill. Not only is it tedious and complicated, but it's also filled with land mines. Take the examples of classroom safety hardware and state-mandated training. The stakes are high—you're dealing with student safety and district compliance with the law. Take, too, Jake's situation. He's been thrown into an outright minefield, and one false step—one injured student, one angry parent, one outraged teacher—can unleash chaos. He could find himself grieved by the union or interrogated by the school board. If he really messes up, he could face disciplinary action or set his career back several years, viewed as totally incompetent by the people in charge.

You signed a contract for one position, and here you are, doing something else entirely. Never in your wildest dreams did you think your job would entail running active shooter training for bus drivers, or helping the operations team with asbestos abatement, or fielding questions about the technological firewall, or recruiting sponsors for your football field, or meeting with the district's lawyers to decide how security cameras should be staged throughout your school, or a hundred other tasks for which you have zero expertise.

If you expect patience and sympathy from your colleagues, think again. "That's admin life," your leader pals will say, before regaling you with some anecdote about the short straws they've drawn. The downsides of "admin life" were hilarious when your buddy had to wear the school mascot costume for Homecoming, but they're not so funny now. Your actions may have financial, legal, or safety implications. You have to get this right or you could end up causing serious damage to other people or to the district.

Nonchalance from your fellow leaders is irritating, but it's nothing compared to what you'll get from teachers, students, and parents: a ruthless demand for competence, regardless of your experience. Everyone from the janitor to the superintendent subscribes to the philosophy that an administrator should know everything. You can try to be transparent and explain that grad school didn't cover every scenario under the sun. You can ask for help, and maybe you can even delegate. Still, though, if you step on one of the land mines, you're on your own.

I know you can't say it, so I will: It's not fair. It is, in fact, completely unjust to find yourself under a trial by fire through no fault of your own. You should not have to catch everyone else's hot potatoes, and "admin life" should not expose you to perilous situations you were never prepared for. You shouldn't have to face other people's callous humor and exacting expectations as you try to manage this task.

But here you are, faced with an important but burdensome project that has nothing to do with your job description. You were never taught to do these things. You have no more expertise than the next person. Yet you drew the short straw somehow, and now people are relying on you to figure it out. So how do you accomplish vital tasks you neither asked for nor are prepared for?

Avoid the Pitfalls
Don't Try to Get Out of It

It won't work. By the time this task lands on your to-do list, it's already been tossed around the upper echelons, and the decision has been made. This can happen to anyone, even those highest on the food chain. Whenever you resent your superintendent for throwing you a curveball, just watch him jump through hoops for the school board. The higher-ups have every right to delegate unpleasant tasks to you, and they're not going to change their mind just because you don't like their decision.

Trying to wriggle out of the project can actually harm you. You know that you'll look lazy and uncooperative if you try to pass a hot potato along, but in the heat of the moment, panic may drive you to throw caution to the wind and make the attempt. You think of how onerous the task is or how unqualified you are to do it, and you instinctively want to duck. Keep that instinct under control by remembering a few facts of admin life:

- **Your reputation is your most valuable asset.** If you build a glowing reputation, others will support you. They'll forgive your mistakes. They'll trust you to run your department your own way. They'll offer you promotions and other leadership opportunities. Life will be better for you. If, however, you build a reputation as lazy, selfish, and truculent, you're sabotaging yourself. Not only will you damage your career prospects but you will also provoke mistrust and resentment from your colleagues. Before you try to get out of a project, think about the damage you will do to your most precious resource.
- **Today impacts tomorrow.** What you do right now, in this moment, will have ripple effects. People will treat you with respect or resentment depending on how you act, and what's more, you will gain more or less power depending on how you handle this task. Trying to get out of the project—or whining about it—could blow up in your face. Once others see you as incompetent, they will deliberately exclude you from major decisions, believing that you don't

want to take on any responsibility. If you somehow successfully worm out of this task, you could be handed an even worse one tomorrow, and you'll certainly provoke the anger of whatever colleague ends up picking up your slack. Think about your future before trying to pass the buck.

- **This could turn out well for you.** When you're staring down the barrel of some onerous task, it's hard to see a golden opportunity, but it's there. If you prove yourself capable of managing even a complex, litigious, unpleasant project that you didn't volunteer for, you'll be entrusted with better projects in the future. When you want to do something your own way, those in power will trust you. When you want more authority, more latitude, you'll get it. When you're looking for a promotion, you can call this example to your aid, reminding everyone how well you handled this high-stakes project.

Don't Phone It In

When mandated to complete some irritating task no one else wanted, you might consider doing the bare minimum, phoning in the faintest effort or handing in some slapdash product. It's not your area of expertise, after all, so no one really expects you to do a good job, right?

Wrong. Everyone from your supervisors to your direct reports expects you to do a good job. Short-straw projects usually have high stakes; this is why no one wants to do them. They tend to be open to public scrutiny and have a lot riding on them, so you have to produce a quality result.

You're not going to do it perfectly on your first try, and you'll have to continually revise your work, but you still have to give this project your best shot. Doing anything less will hurt yourself—and possibly others. Crucial projects related to security, finances, union negotiations, board relations, school staffing, and legal compliance have domino effects, so a perfunctory performance simply isn't an option. When the devil on your shoulder urges you to throw something together just to check this task off your list, remember what's at stake for you, your staff, and your students.

Navigate a Path
Control the Narrative

You're going to be under a microscope no matter what, so make sure you're the one twirling the dials.

The best way to control the narrative around the project is to involve other people. You can't pawn the whole project off on them or force them to shoulder your responsibility, but you can solicit their advice to keep the work on track. Make a list of what you need to learn, then find those who have the knowledge you lack. Jake, for example, will want to enlist the help of key staff members at the elementary school. He can set up meetings with the school psychologist to learn about behavioral policies, the food service team to learn about lunch orders, the secretary to learn about parent communication, and more. He'd also be wise to establish a standing meeting with another elementary principal to get extra guidance as he ventures into the unknown. In the process, he will gather advice in addition to acquiring information. He needs to know what to do and how to do it successfully in this interim role—for instance, he'll need to know the school discipline policy as well as how to explain and defend it to parents.

Your situation might not be so clear-cut. You might be creating something from nothing—perhaps you have to invent a program or policy from scratch. You could also be navigating state and federal laws or walking the tightrope of local politics. Trickiest of all, you might be trying to build a product that satisfies everyone from the union to the superintendent to the school board. You have no chance of success unless you involve others.

You might fear that you will lose control over the narrative by bringing other people into the mix, but it's the other way around. You lose control when no one knows what you're doing because people fill in the gaps with their own, often ungenerous, speculation. If you work in isolation, you will take 100 percent of the blame when others find fault with your product—and unless you have discovered the key to pleasing everyone, others will inevitably find faults. If, however, you've involved representatives from all stakeholders, you can add their voices to yours when you explain how and why you created it. You can justify collaborative decisions and praise your colleagues' insight. People might still hate the end result, but they can't accuse you of forging ahead on your own.

Enlisting other people helps you control the narrative by demonstrating how cooperative, conscientious, and thorough you are. "I'm not an expert, so I found some people who are," you can say, explaining how you consulted those with the skills and knowledge you lack, or "This project will impact our faculty, so I recruited some teachers to help me make a solid plan." It's true that you're handling something foreign to you, but far from looking incompetent, you will look capable. You've shifted the narrative from "I drew the short straw and suffered through it" to "This amazing team has created a wonderful plan."

Enlisting other people also maintains an agreeable narrative for your stakeholders. As you consult more and more people, you'll learn what land mines to avoid and what nonnegotiables to protect. You will, in fact, do a better job than you would in isolation. Look at Jake. Meeting with the psychologist, secretary, and food service team to learn how the school works will make him much more effective than he would otherwise be—and people will notice. His staff will see how diligently he's trying to learn the ropes, and they will talk about his efforts rather than his failings. When you're creating something from scratch, show your drafts, ideas, and theories to as many people as possible before declaring the project finished. That way, your end product will be more likely to go over well as you avert disasters and even add flourishes to make it more appealing.

In a similar vein, you can control the narrative through meticulous documentation and verification. If this project involves a presentation phase—for example, if you have to create and roll out a new policy—documenting the process is just as important as the end product. You will need to explain and maybe defend your process, so make sure it can stand up to scrutiny. Document every conversation or meeting, however informal. Did you call the district attorney to check the wording of a law? Write up a summary of your conversation. Did you get a panel of teachers together to think through the impact of your project? Keep an annotated meeting agenda. Track every last one of your sources and cite all research, laws, surveys, and data that went into your decisions.

If documentation is your armor, verification is your sword. With every step you take, run your progress past whoever handed you the task. If they offer to meet with you for status updates and problem-solving, take them up on it; this gets you facetime with someone who can correct you if you're going off course and help you forge a better end result. If the higher-up in question is too busy for meetings or has no interest in discussing a tedious task, you'll have to be creative to verify your progress with them. Email regular status updates to establish written evidence of communication that you gave your boss ample opportunity to intervene. When you see them in passing, find an excuse to chat about the project, especially if it means getting a green light for your work or an answer to a question they've been ignoring. You might feel like a pest, but you have to get their eyes and ears on your work.

Documenting and verifying your every move will help control the narrative around the short straw you drew. It turns your work into a public record, available for anyone to examine and open for your boss to correct. You will establish yourself as transparent, collaborative, and eager to learn rather than nervous, secretive, and eager to get things over with. Plainly put, you'll cover your backside and ensure that the task is done right.

Turn Critics into Comrades

The worst thing about short straws is that no one wants to do them but everyone has an opinion about how they should be done. Draw the short straw, and suddenly, you're onstage facing a tomato-wielding audience.

Short-straw tasks attract legions of critics precisely *because* they're important. Everyone agrees on the criticality of social media policies and school safety protocols, for instance, but they would never put themselves forward to lead such sticky undertakings unless it was part of their job description. When they find out, however, that someone else drew the short straw, they are free to bestow their sage advice on the poor sucker, perhaps sharing the latest headlines on teachers who posted inappropriate photos or warnings about inadequate lockdown procedures.

Knowing that everyone and their mother wants to register an opinion, your only option is to turn your critics into comrades. You won't transform them by pulling a perfect result out of a hat—in fact, your end product will inevitably irritate *someone*. Instead, you turn critics into comrades by winning them over as you work, which builds on your efforts to control the narrative. You might already be asking for guidance and input as you involve others in the project; now take it a step farther by deliberately investigating pressure points, which usually include the following:

- **Emotional baggage**—the fears and feelings swirling around the project. In the case of a social media policy, for example, staff might fear having their every post monitored by vindictive parents or colleagues.
- **Historical trauma**—the reasons this project has been kicked down the road for so long. In the case of an updated safety protocol, for instance, there may have been several poor protocols in place already, each one less effective than the last.
- **Political danger**—the labyrinth of internal and external factions demanding nonnegotiable outcomes. The union, parent groups, school board, and state legislature are probably just a few of the factions tugging on the corners of short-straw projects.

Pressure points are the reason people become critical. When others fear you're going to make life worse for them or repeat historical missteps, they will jump in to offer what they see as indispensable advice—and what you experience as captious badgering. The key to turning critics into comrades is to learn as much as possible about their pressure points. As they line up to nitpick your work or dole out unsolicited advice, resist the urge to run away. Instead, ask question after question with the intent of discovering and disarming pressure points: What are the most widespread fears and feelings, and where did they come from? What has gone wrong with prior efforts? What are the non-negotiable demands from the union, the school board, and other stakeholders, and what's open to discussion?

You will turn some critics into comrades simply by listening to their perspective. These people don't necessarily want to be involved in the decision-making process—they just want to be heard. Show that you understand their viewpoint before, during, and after you complete your work, even (and especially) if you can't give them exactly what they want. They will appreciate your acknowledgment of their perspective.

Other critics want to directly influence whatever project or policy you're working on. Sometimes these are people whose grievances necessitated your task—you might, for instance, find yourself revamping library policies with the very parents who complained about them at last week's board meeting—so earning their support is imperative. Here's the catch: You can't necessarily give these critics everything they want. If it were that easy, someone else would have done it. Since you won't be able to fulfill their every wish, you might be tempted to sway them with sympathy: "I *totally* agree with you, but I'm completely powerless here." That approach won't work. It pits them against some malevolent force hell-bent on ruining their ideas and implies that resolution is impossible. (It's also rather cowardly.)

Turning these people into comrades starts in your mind: You have to view them as your teammates and allies, challenging though it may be. You must convey the belief that, together, you will find an answer and that you are glad to have the invaluable resource of thoughtful experts at your side. You also have to let them see the complicated quagmire of the situation and try their hand at solving problems. Let's say, for instance, you're working with the union, which is complaining that the school doesn't take student misbehavior seriously enough. The first step is to put them in a room with the district's lawyer and a state board of education representative so that you can all discuss the laws surrounding student discipline with ample information on the table. Then, share the school staffing budget to see whether new dean positions are even possible. Finally, bring in parent representatives so you can gauge how the community would respond to new disciplinary policies. With this approach, the union doesn't have to take your word for what "can" and "can't" be done, and you're not constantly on the defensive, batting away their demands because you alone know what's realistic. Once they see the big picture for themselves, all of you can have a productive, nuanced discussion grounded in reality.

If you treat your critics like children to be pacified, they might act like children when they don't get what they want. If, however, you treat them like intelligent adults who are capable of grasping nuance, they will eventually appreciate the complexity of the situation. Even if they aren't totally satisfied with your end product, they will understand the complications and compromises that went into its creation. They'll feel a sense of camaraderie with you now that you've involved them in weighty decisions. You're not surrendering to their every whim, but you're also not shielding them from the gnarly truth; you're enlisting them as fully informed teammates who, like you, will have to negotiate to a consensus.

You need comrades, especially as people queue up to criticize your work on a project you never wanted. Recruit from that queue of critics, because those people know what's at stake with your work at least as well as you do, and they can be powerful allies if you earn their support by trusting them with the full truth.

Leverage Your Success

Short-straw projects may feel like a pebble in your shoe, but you can make them a feather in your cap. If you have successfully controlled the narrative around the project, demonstrating your collaboration skills, your diligent documentation, and your transparency with stakeholders, you've already laid a strong foundation. Add the critics you've won over, and you have all the ingredients you need to turn this short straw into a crown jewel such as a promotion, a raise, or simply more bargaining power. Maybe you want people to trust you with better projects or more funding. Maybe you want more control over your department and less micromanaging from your boss. Do a short-straw project well, and you can earn any of these perks.

There's an advertising element at play here. Completing a thankless task in secret will serve your kids and school, but it might not do your career aspirations much good. It can be tricky to find ways to share your success without appearing eager for a gold star. One simple way to showcase your successful handling of a project is to constantly express gratitude for what you learned and *especially* for those who helped you learn it. Being a reflective practitioner who acknowledges the contributions of others will benefit both you and your reputation. You can also cast a positive light on any mistakes you made while managing the short-straw project. Jake, for example, doesn't describe his time as interim kindergarten principal as a harrowing ordeal but as a learning experience made all the richer by the best staff in the world: "You know, I used to think I knew all the ins and outs of how the district ran, but boy, did I get a wake-up call at Central School! Every day I learned something new, and the staff were so patient with me. They showed me how to handle discipline, ordering, parent communication, and more. Thanks to them, I feel like a different person now—like I'm a hundred times more capable than I was three months ago. We really do have an amazing team here."

Another way to leverage your success is to refer to the skills it took to handle the short straw when you are vying for better projects. If, say, you were ordered to sit on a tedious state licensure committee, you can cite your increased knowledge of licensing requirements when proposing ways to address your district's teacher shortage. If you were forced to become a certified trainer for some mandatory district program, you can cite your presentation skills when trying to instill your own professional development ideas. Jake, whose only administrative role was math coordinator, can now cite building leadership experience when applying for assistant superintendent; he is certainly more prepared to manage high-stakes tasks now that he has led at both the building and the district level. This learning is the proverbial silver lining; no matter how irritating or involuntary, experience is experience. It's all fair game when you need to showcase your skills.

The final way to leverage your success after pulling and handling a short straw is to maintain the network you've built in the process. You probably had to manage internal committees, schmooze external stakeholders, or, if that straw was *really* short, enlist legal or state guidance. Don't let the connections go to waste. Whatever relationships you've built, maintain them. Drop by the classrooms or offices of people from your district just to say hello. Keep in touch with external contacts via social media or email. You learned from and supported one another and can continue to do so, but it's more than that. As we've seen, your reputation is your most important asset, and you want everyone who witnessed your work on the project to think and speak well of you. Keeping those relationships alive is essential. If, say, you found yourself working with parent liaisons while handling the project, check in with them a few weeks after the project is finished to see how they perceive the end product. This simple act will nurture the relationship that will not only help both of you be stronger, more supportive educational advocates but also polish your reputation as a conscientious, thoughtful leader—which could pay off when you're up for a promotion or need some social capital to cash in.

Other people may feel a guilty gratitude when *you* draw the short straw, knowing *they* don't have to worry about it. In contrast, your open gratitude will propel you to better positions or projects. Do it right—advertise your success, cite your experience, and maintain your network—and you can actually use this cumbersome task to grow and enhance your professional prospects.

In Summary

Handling an excruciating task that has nothing to do with your job description is an unfortunate reality of administrative life. It may throw your skill and knowledge gaps into sharp relief, making you wonder whether you missed a course in grad school or whether you're just incompetent. The system treats administrators as convenient fodder to throw at any odd job, regardless of experience, then holds them accountable for doing the task well on the first attempt. When you draw the short straw, you might consider trying to get out of it or phoning in your performance, but don't. You'll only make yourself look lazy and irresponsible. Instead, focus on **controlling the narrative** around the project, modeling transparency and collaboration to all stakeholders, including and especially your boss. Then, **turn critics into comrades** by bringing them into the process—or even just listening to them. Most importantly, make sure to **leverage your success** with the project, perhaps to take a step up the ladder or simply to have more operational independence. Even if you doubt your ability to create a perfect product, it's essential to make sure that your process shows your growth and showcases you in the best light.

7

The Instructional Impostor

Shonda dreads the sight of a blank page. No, she's not a novelist—she's an assistant principal with 10 years of administrative experience, but those classroom feedback forms intimidate her every time. She diligently visits every class in her large high school so that she can evaluate teachers from all subject areas and provide feedback, as she is trained to do.

That training, though, must have been missing a piece because Shonda feels like an impostor. Who is she to give instructional feedback to these teachers? Why should they take advice from her? She taught for seven years—enough to earn tenure and learn the ropes—but still far less than many of the teachers in her school. Dozens of teachers under her supervision are now in their 20th year or beyond, which makes her feel her classroom experience pales in comparison.

On top of that, she only taught science but now finds herself evaluating teachers of math, language, history, art, and other subjects she hasn't studied for decades. Busy as she is, Shonda isn't able to attend professional development for every subject to learn the latest pedagogical techniques, so she feels unsure of what to look for from classroom to classroom. Moreover, her extensive administrative career is beginning to work against her; with every passing year, she grows more removed from the classroom, and teachers know it. She gets the impression that her staff view her as slightly out of touch because she hasn't actually taught for over a decade.

Shonda doesn't dare voice any of these doubts. She can hear her principal now: "Good teaching is good teaching. The core pillars of solid instruction don't change from grade to grade or subject to subject, and anyway, the Danielson Framework for Teaching provides a clear picture of what classrooms should look like." That's the party line. It's also why Shonda can't admit to feeling like a phony: If she confesses to being out of her depth, other leaders will think she doesn't know good teaching when she sees it. Obviously, she knows good teaching, but that only makes it harder to give feedback to the many excellent teachers in her building. Most of them are more skilled than she ever was, and she often struggles to think of guidance beyond "Great lesson."

Shonda knows it's her job as an instructional leader to improve teaching and learning, and she tries to coach teachers with confidence. After all, teachers expect her to be knowledgeable and helpful, and she has a responsibility to them. Walking around saying, "Sorry, I can't help you with math instruction" or "I can't think of anything, so I guess you're doing well enough" would be a dereliction of duty. On the other hand, Shonda doesn't want to come off as brash, throwing around poorly informed advice just to appear clever. Teachers would see right through that, and consequently would have less trust in her. Every time she visits a classroom, every time she completes an evaluation, Shonda doubts her abilities.

Debrief the Doubts

Feeling like an instructional impostor is the least acknowledged trigger of doubt among educational leaders, and for good reason. Would you *ever* tell a colleague you didn't feel confident providing instructional feedback? Only if you want to pack it up in June. Providing instructional feedback is your main responsibility—chances are, it's literally in your job description. Your reputation as a leader hinges on your ability to lead pedagogical reform in your building. Like all districts, yours upholds the idea that, because you completed your teacher evaluation training, you are an expert in all things instructional.

Between you and me, though, it's normal to doubt your ability to provide useful instructional feedback to every teacher in every scenario. Even if you taught for decades before stepping into leadership, the second you leave your classroom, you start to lose the view from the trenches. You might not forget the important aspects of planning, classroom management, and so on, but you will inevitably have to direct teachers to do things you never had to do: follow new rules, embrace new methods, master new technology, complete new paperwork, develop new mindsets, and more. When you do, you'll likely feel a mixture of guilt and fraudulence as you push initiatives that never applied to you.

Then there's the possibility that you supervise teachers who teach different subjects or grade levels than you did—former high school teachers can become kindergarten principals, after all. We all know that "good teaching is good teaching," a tautology we theoretically embrace to ease our entry into unfamiliar classrooms. You've probably had this and other unassailable viewpoints, such as "The basic principles of teaching and learning are consistent across subjects and grade levels" or "Effective instruction has never been more clearly defined than it is now, thanks to the Danielson Framework," drilled into you by well-meaning mentors.

If you're like me, such platitudes inflame your doubts rather than allay them. You might fear that if you can't provide useful feedback in every classroom, every time, you are an ignoramus who knows nothing about teaching after all. Galloping behind that fear is the dread of being exposed as a charlatan, a poser who cheated their way into leadership. *That teacher will see right through me,* you think, as you rummage around your brain trying to find something constructive to say to the veteran instructor leading a masterful lesson before your eyes. *They're a better teacher than I ever was, but somehow, I'm the boss. I'm a total fake.*

Your doubts aren't totally baseless. If teachers see you as out of your depth, they will, in fact, lose some confidence in you. Why wouldn't they? They teach. Their friends teach. The guy down the hall teaches. Teaching is a demanding profession that they tackle every day. They expect you to tackle it with them, even when that means facing your own learning curve. Your pedagogical skills might come up short—a fact that hurts to admit. To make matters worse, the best teachers in your building are *always* the most eager for feedback, aren't they? Meeting with a virtuoso who is begging you to help them improve can make you feel completely exposed.

We administrators face the formidable task of continuing to improve our instructional skills long after leaving the classroom despite not having the time, training, or arena in which to do so. That conflict is what's behind all this doubt: We are working to guide those who do something that we no longer do. So how do you provide instructional leadership for teachers who are out of your lane—and sometimes out of your league?

Avoid the Pitfalls

Don't Nitpick for Lack of Real Suggestions

"Well, you've got all the big stuff down, but the flag was crooked."

When observing an absolute powerhouse in the classroom, you might feel so stumped, so unqualified to give constructive feedback, that you resort to nitpicking. Your brain somehow makes the logical leap that the feedback continuum starts with "big things" and ends with "little things," but challenge that assumption. No one masters all the big things simultaneously—if ever—and depending on each teacher's unique style, the little things might not have any effect on the overall instruction. That's why those rock star teachers don't respond well to caviling over minutia.

If teachers find nitpicking useless (and annoying), why do it? It accomplishes nothing—least of all improved instruction—and it damages your relationship with the teacher. Giving in to this particular urge works against everything you want to achieve with your classroom observations.

If you're trying to decide whether a comment is nitpicky, ask yourself the following questions:

- Would taking my suggestion have a direct, obvious impact on student learning, behavior, or well-being?
- Does my suggestion reinforce expectations that I have clearly communicated?
- Is what I'm advising completely within the teacher's control?

If the answer to all three questions is yes, you can safely make your recommendation without fear of splitting hairs. If the answer to one or more is no, go back to the drawing board.

Don't Punt by Claiming Inexperience

You think you're being candid, vulnerable, relatable by demurring. "I'm just saying; I'm not a math person, you know?" you say to the math teacher you're evaluating, hoping the two of you can share a laugh over this gap in your skill set. It feels like a friendly way to admit to your lack of experience, and you congratulate yourself on your humility.

Although you don't want to pretend to have experience you didn't earn—teachers, like everyone else, tend to frown on lying—you also don't want to bury your credibility under an avalanche of self-deprecation. Moreover, your inexperience doesn't let you off the hook. You still have to generate helpful feedback for teachers even if you never taught their particular subject or grade level, and even if they have 20 years' more experience than you. Beginning by lowering expectations looks like you're trying to get out of doing your job.

Punting by claiming lack of experience also makes you appear unwilling to learn, which sets a bad example. Let's say you're a former elementary teacher now in your first administrative job as a middle school assistant principal. During those first months, you might feel out of your depth as you watch classrooms that look and feel nothing like those from your previous life, but it's simply not an option to tell your staff, "Don't expect much from me. I'm an elementary ed person." At least, go with, "Every day, I learn more and more about middle school just by soaking in the expertise I witness in your classrooms." If you act like you don't have to adapt, adjust, and grow, you give teachers an excuse not to do those very things, which will make school improvement borderline impossible.

Navigate a Path
Spend Plenty of Time Just Watching

Spend time observing classrooms and teachers. Not making suggestions, not monitoring for compliance, not trying to identify the "good" teachers—just watching. That line about "soaking in the expertise"? This is the part where you actually do it. Set a goal for yourself: Aim to do a certain number of classroom observations each week, spend a certain number of hours in subjects you're least familiar with, or visit every classroom in the school a certain number of times each month. Whatever your goal, track your progress in a visible location so you're always aware of how you're doing.

You might spend a few weeks or even a few months just watching, depending on how much you need to learn. Either way, be open with teachers. If they know you're observing them for your own growth, they'll wait more patiently for you to help them with theirs. They'll respect your determination to learn first, then speak. As you talk with your staff, rephrase those self-effacing punts as confident statements of eagerness, combined with questions that honor teachers' expertise. See Figure 7.1 for a few examples.

By turning statements of uncertainty into statements of eagerness, you communicate the expectation that you *will* learn. You *will* develop the required expertise. Your learning journey has a clear destination, and you're going to reach it. This allows you to model professional growth for your staff by demonstrating the most valuable ability of all: learning new skills throughout your career.

The questions built into those rephrased punts serve two purposes: They build your relationships with the teachers and they help you learn. When you ask teachers for their insight, you honor their expertise. You demonstrate such regard for their instructional skill that, in fact, you trust them to instruct you—their boss.

Some leaders fear this idea, believing that asking a teacher to explain a concept is tantamount to admitting weakness, but

Figure 7.1. Rephrase to Communicate Confidence

Instead of...	Try...
"I taught English for 10 years, but science totally scares me. This covalent bond stuff is going to go right over my head."	"I'm so excited to delve into more science rooms! It's been a while since I studied chemistry, but that just means I can really put myself into your students' shoes. Do you mind if I sit with them while they're doing the lab so I can interact with them and with the learning materials?"
"I'm not an elementary ed person, so I'm really not sure what to look for here."	"I'm learning so much during my first month here at Smith Elementary! The biggest surprise for me was the emphasis elementary teachers place on routines. Can you walk me through what you do to keep your routines running so smoothly?"
"Honestly, I'm not sure what to say. You're such a fantastic teacher, I don't know if I have anything valuable to offer you."	"That was amazing. I want to make sure I'm offering you valuable feedback, so can you tell me a bit more about what you'd find useful? For instance, are you working toward any particular personal goals? Would you like me to gather some student perspectives so that we can talk about them?"

it's all in the delivery. When, for example, you ask an elementary teacher to walk you through classroom routines, your tone should say, "I'm so fascinated and eager," not "I'm so stupid and embarrassed." If you're afraid of looking weak asking a teacher to explain something, just think of how weak you'll look when you can't participate in instructional conversations because you know nothing about their approach to instruction. You won't be able to competently participate in professional learning communities, curricular discussion, or pedagogical planning, and teachers will notice. If, on the other hand, you've learned what you need to about unfamiliar subjects or levels, you'll become a respected instructional leader in your building.

Consider, too, how it would appear to keep showing up in classrooms without providing feedback *and* without engaging teachers in conversation. It would be creepy. You'd be the silent specter looming in the background, and teachers would dread your visits because they'd never know what you were thinking. If you're not there to evaluate, monitor, or provide feedback, make your visit purposeful by striking up a conversation with the goal of learning something from the teacher. If there isn't an appropriate moment to do so while you're in the room, do it as soon as possible afterward. Seek the teacher out later that day, expressing gratitude and eagerness: "Jim, I loved being in your second period! Tell me more about paired verbal fluency—I've never seen that technique in action." The key is to get teachers to open up about their planning and delivery so you can learn from them. This will empower you to see behind the scenes of otherwise foreign-looking lessons.

The more you watch, the more you'll learn, and you'll soon have both the knowledge and relationships to provide solid guidance.

Start with the Students

When you feel ready to give feedback, start by applying a general lens to the students, not the teacher. In other words, watch and listen to the students, running their actions through the filter of what you've discovered in your weeks or months of observations. If you learned, for instance, the essentials of inquiry-based learning by watching the science department, keep your eyes open for student curiosity and questioning. Capture exact quotes from students. How do they discuss their learning? Do they express wonderment, excitement, and interest?

Other lenses might include interactions between students, student time on task, or student–teacher talk ratio. You could specifically attend to student behavior or adherence to routines. You could analyze students' use of instructional technology. You could even spend time talking to students, if you can do so without disrupting the lesson. When I was a teacher, I had a principal who spent every classroom visit asking my students what they were learning in my class and why. He would transcribe their answers and pass them along to me, verbatim, so we could analyze together how students experienced my class based on their own comments rather than his subjective interpretation. This practice was invaluable. Focusing on pure and simple facts—quotes, numbers, and so on—helped us start the conversation on an even footing.

The goal is to collect student-focused observations that can generate productive conversations with teachers without requiring any judgment from you. Shonda, for example, might use concrete observational data such as the following to start conversations with teachers from every department in her high school:

- "Anna, I wrote down some really impassioned quotes from students during that debate on modern politics during your third hour. My favorite one was 'Border security is a moral imperative.' How do you inspire such verve in students? Are there any kids you're still trying to get more invested in the issues?"
- "Kyle, I heard 12 out of the 20 students in your French class respond to questions in French at least once during your lesson. Tell me, when is it appropriate for students to speak English, and when do you insist on maintaining the French environment?"

- "Yesenia, I noticed that all except two students finished the quiz quickly, and you let those two work for another 10 minutes before resuming instruction for the class. What's your thought process for timing your assessments?"

If you're a seasoned evaluator, the focus on numbers, quotes, and objective evidence probably sounds familiar as the basis for rating lessons. However, you can use student-based observations for anything you like, including simply striking up a conversation, building a relationship, or learning about instruction. In the quotes above, notice the opportunities for Shonda to provide feedback if the conversation heads in that direction. She might brainstorm ways for Anna to bring the quiet students into the debate or suggest post-quiz activities for Yesenia's students to complete while their peers are still working. She's not just jumping in with a pile of suggestions, though; she's inviting the teacher to join her in a discussion of evidence. Starting with an observation and following it with a question that respects the teacher's skill makes space for a nuanced discussion.

You don't have to amass copious evidence during every casual walk-through, nor should you instigate a deep dialogue while a teacher is trying to run their class, but if you're trying to overcome instructional impostor syndrome, start with the students. By providing an unbiased student snapshot, you open the door to a conversation the teacher cares about, even if that conversation has to wait until after class. You also build your credibility as an instructional leader and shore up your own confidence in coaching teachers.

Ask Reflective Questions

Reflection is one of the best drivers of professional growth. You can write pages and pages of insightful feedback, bombarding your staff with your abundant knowledge, but it won't change a thing unless teachers reflect on it. It's their prerogative to accept or reject your advice. If you want them to accept it, you need to trigger reflection. Reflection connects our past actions to our present reality. For instance, it might help a teacher see how ignoring classroom routines for months has resulted in a chaotic environment. It can also uncover aspirations we never consciously examined, such as a desire to be able to joke around more with students. Although some teachers reflect regularly on their own, everyone benefits from a nudge, especially from a trusted colleague. That's where you come in.

It's best to ask reflective questions in person. Avoid the usual evaluation trip wire of "How do you think the lesson went?" which usually prompts the unreflective response "Pretty well." Avoid, too, any reflective question that essentially boils down to, "How could you do better?" Instead, try to ask about something you observed while visiting the classroom. You can build on the idea of starting with the students or ask a question about the teacher's actions. Either way, you're trying to get teachers to think creatively by providing a fresh set of eyes. Here are some examples:

- "Maria, your students' discussion of the novel showed high levels of interest—they really care about these characters! How did you generate that enthusiasm, and what are your plans for leveraging it?"
- "Jamal, you used several types of questions throughout the lesson, including everything from basic recall to high-level analysis. What questioning techniques get your students most engaged?"

These questions have a double benefit: They help the teacher reflect, and they help you learn from the teacher's thought process and explanation, countering feelings of instructional inadequacy as you evaluate work in an unfamiliar domain.

You can add reflective questions to written feedback, but if you do, make sure to clarify the purpose of the questions and what you expect from teachers. If teachers receive a written feedback form with a reflective query, they might assume they have to answer it in writing, which just adds to their pile of work. If the question sounds judgmental, they might get defensive ("Of course I thought about that idea. *I did it right before you walked in!*"). Some teachers receive written questions in the spirit they're intended, but to others, they're an annoyance. Be judicious and aware, and if a teacher tells you they feel pressured to reply to your written questions, maybe forgo them for that particular person.

Ask for Feedback on Your Feedback

Seeking teachers' reactions to my feedback didn't even occur to me until several years into my administrative career. If, as a newbie, I had realized I could ask teachers how helpful my feedback was, I would have improved so much faster. I'm sure I would have received different answers from different people, but to be fair, teachers deal with that all the time: One supervisor thinks they're perfect, the next picks them apart. Some kids love them, some kids hate them. If teachers can deal with the maddening array of responses, so can you. That said, you may discover trends in the feedback your teachers give you that will help you identify overall areas in which you can make your comments more helpful.

Start with the teachers you have trusting relationships with. Ask them for feedback on your feedback and be open to their responses. The more specific your questions, the more detailed their responses will be. For example:

- "What are the most and least helpful pieces of feedback I've given you?"

- "Do you gain any insight from student quotes? If so, what are some questions I could ask them that would spark answers that are useful to you?"
- "How helpful is it when I count the number of students doing a given activity?"
- "Do you find value in reflective questions, even when they're in writing?"
- "Is there something in particular you want me to look for and comment on while I'm in your room? For instance, are you working toward any personal goals?"
- "Do you mind when I interact with your students, assuming I'm not interrupting instruction?"

Some of these questions ask about personal preferences, so it's possible that you will get a variety of answers that prompt you to tailor your feedback to the teacher you're observing. For instance, you might ask Mr. Smith reflective questions but leave them off Ms. Rowman's form. Even if you can't accommodate everyone's preference, there is value in receiving teachers' feedback because it might reveal trends and areas to improve. For example, you might be determined to interact with students in every classroom, but if multiple teachers say your volume as you talk to students is distracting, you know what aspect of your practice to adjust. You might notice most teachers asking for feedback on a new initiative—the new technology platform or the new phonics program, for instance—and get a sense of how teachers are feeling about the change.

Asking for feedback on your feedback proves yourself open, flexible, and willing to grow—the very qualities you wish to foster in your staff. It will engender trust between you and teachers and develop your skill as an instructional leader in your building.

In Summary

Leaders may not exactly *do* what their teams do—after all, baseball coaches don't have to hit home runs—but they must be able to help their teams improve. That's why feeling like an instructional impostor is particularly terrifying: It intensifies your own doubt that you might not be cut out for this job. When you observe teachers working in subjects or grade levels you never taught, it's tempting to cover your inexperience with self-effacing punts. On the other hand, watching teachers who are completely out of your league leaves you speechless, unable to offer a single useful suggestion. Rather than resort to nitpicking, dodging, or hiding in your office, work on building your observational skills slowly. When you're in classrooms, **spend plenty of time just watching**, without providing feedback. Do this for several weeks or even months. This practice serves the dual purpose of building relationships with staff and allowing you to learn more about areas that are new to you. When you're ready to give feedback, **start with the students**; their learning, behavior, and well-being are of interest to every teacher. **Ask reflective questions** designed to spark teachers' insight and ideas. If you're willing to be vulnerable, **ask for feedback on your feedback** and look for trends in what teachers tell you. If you secretly feel like a fraud when you watch instruction, there is a way out. Commit to developing your skill without denigrating your capacity to grow.

Conclusion

Self-doubt is natural at the best of times. Given everything educational leaders face today, it's downright inevitable. Staff morale is low, turnover is high, and even seemingly trivial problems have the potential to spiral into crises. If you find yourself doubting your ability to survive—let alone thrive—as an educational leader right now, know that you're not alone.

More important, *you're not broken*. Self-doubt isn't a symptom of incompetence or poor professional fit. On the contrary, it's an indication of a reflective practitioner. It suggests you know how high the stakes are for yourself, your staff, and your students, and you want to do your best—despite everything. That's why you shouldn't treat doubt as a syndrome to manage or a shameful secret. You don't need to "fix" yourself. The problem isn't in your head—it's out there, in a system that places more and more pressure on you to combat injustice, inspire joy, juggle politics, reduce attrition, and solve every social ill under the sun, all with a smile on your face. Doubting your ability to meet these extreme demands is perfectly reasonable. It would, in fact, be rather alarming to see any leader face these pressures with blind hubris.

Rather than entertain the unhelpful question of whether you're cut out for educational leadership, focus on how you respond to situations that inflame your doubt. You want to not only be prepared—and hopefully this book helps you feel so—but also spend time reflecting on the ways you succeed despite your doubts. Every time you successfully manage an angry mob, every time you competently sell a contentious change, and every time you deftly handle a short-straw project, you gain additional evidence that you are a skillful leader. Reflect on this evidence when your dubious internal monologue tells you you're not cut out to be a leader. Understand that doubt itself isn't a saboteur, it's a whetstone. Your doubts (perhaps acknowledged only to yourself) didn't blow everything up, they honed your skills—and you thrived. They may even have spurred you to greater excellence by prompting you to think deeply and act deliberately.

Of course, reflection is useful to you, but you can make your experience useful to others by sharing it. If you're tired of feeling guilty, hiding your doubts, and suspecting a "real" leader would be more confident, your next step is clear: Break the silence. Be open about your experience with self-doubt so others know they're not alone. Start small, if you like, by confiding in your most trusted colleagues during a crisis of confidence. You'll likely find that they respond with such empathy for you and gratitude for your openness that you'll feel emboldened to keep going. When a colleague draws the short straw on a project you know they're unprepared for, share your own experience feeling cold terror and facing it down. When you see a friend downcast after the boss's screaming session, take the first step and empathize with their plight, perhaps describing how you faced a similar situation. With every open conversation you have, you chip away at the professional stigma surrounding self-doubt.

Although crises make us feel isolated in the moment, paralyzed with fear and unable to disclose our feelings, the irony is that most crises are quite commonplace. If the scenarios in this book resonated with you, you can be sure that they resonate with others as well. Every educational leader in the country has probably faced all seven scenarios in the first few years on the job, and it's a pity we don't seize opportunities to empathize with one another more. We could be making connections, bonding over our shared experiences, and generating the best responses in collaboration. Crises could bring us together if we talked about them productively. It's not enough to say, "Leading innovation is tough, but capable leaders develop this skill." Such language evokes the idea that you have "it" or you don't. If, on the other hand, we explicitly acknowledge the self-doubt we experience when trying to transform a school or district, we can have a more fruitful conversation—one leading to positive personal development rather than guilt and anxiety.

I also suspect that leaders who openly discuss self-doubt are less likely to leave the profession than those who hide it like a shameful secret. Our backs are already straining under the burden of social and political demands; pressure to project confidence is often the straw that breaks them. We need honest, empathetic discourse, not taboos and restrictions, to keep us strong. The job may feel, if not easier, than certainly more manageable if we can express our doubts without fear of judgment.

Every time a colleague reaches out to say, "I know what you're going through. I've been there myself," I feel myself getting stronger. (I may cry at first, but *then* I get stronger, I swear.) It's the difference between climbing a mountain alone and climbing it with others. If I know other people are there, anchoring me, I'll stay on that mountain and persevere until I get to the top.

References

Bays, C., Thomas, C., Kelly, J. (Writers), & Fryman, P. (Director). (2008, April 14). The chain of screaming (Season 3, Episode 15) [TV series episode]. In C. Bays, P. Fryman, & C. Thomas (Executive Producers), *How I met your mother*. Bays Thomas Productions; 20th Century Fox Television.

Brown, B. (2018.) *Dare to lead: Brave work, tough conversations, whole hearts*. Random House.

Levin, S., & Bradley, K. (2019). *Understanding and addressing principal turnover: A review of the research*. National Association of Secondary School Principals; Learning Policy Institute. https://www.nassp.org/wp-content/uploads/2020/05/nassp_edit06-WEB-1.pdf

Lewis, C. S. (1952). *Mere Christianity*. MacMillan.

National Association of Secondary School Principals. (2021, December 8). *NASSP survey signals a looming mass exodus of principals from schools*. https://www.nassp.org/news/nassp-survey-signals-a-looming-mass-exodus-of-principals-from-schools/

Patterson, K., Grenny, J., Maxfield, D., McMillan, R., & Switzler, A. (2013). *Crucial accountability: Tools for resolving violated expectations, broken commitments, and bad behavior*. McGraw-Hill.

Sudeikis, J., Lawrence, B., Hunt, B. (Writers), & Lowney, D. (Director). (2020, September 18). The Diamond Dogs (Season 1, Episode 8) [TV series episode]. In B. Lawrence, J. Sudeikis, & B. Wrubel (Executive Producers), *Ted Lasso*. Ruby's Tuna; Doozer; Warner Bros. Television.

Wiseman, L. (2017). *Multipliers: How the best leaders make everyone smarter*. HarperBusiness.

Index

accountability, 22
affirmations, 3
agreement, benefits of, 50–52
attribution error, 53
authority, displaying, 34–35

boss's punching bag
    perception as reality, 48, 55–59
    you as the, 44–47
boss's punching bag, avoiding becoming the
    build political credit, 62
    collect facts, 47
    cover your assets, 61
    document, 61–62
    don't assume your boss is entirely wrong or right, 47–49
    don't react emotionally, 49–50
boss's punching bag, navigating a path to defuse fury
    ask yourself why a reasonable person would act this way, 52–55
    document and share progress, 56
    express as much agreement as you can, 50–52
    manage up, 59–63
    prioritize fixing the problem, 55–59

chain of screaming, 46
change. *See* selling change
clear is kind, 22
collaboration, selling the, 16–19
communication
    empathy and, 33–34
    navigating mobs, 79–81, 93–101
    nonverbal, 100–101
cover your assets (CYA), 61
curious, staying, 23–24, 95–96

document and share progress, when to, 56, 61–62
doubt
    elements underlying, 2, 43
    reflecting on, purpose of, 139–140
    shame associated with, 4
    universality of, 4

emotional intelligence, 40–43
emotions
    aspired to, defining, 42
    authority in curbing, 34–35
    choice in responding to, 41–42
    doubt and, 43
    overpowering, responding to, 33–34, 37
    reacting with, 49–50
empathizer, the empty, 28–30

empathy
    excusing vs., 39
    in theory vs. practice, 30–33
empathy, avoiding the pitfalls of
    don't speak until you have control, 33–34
    don't throw your authority around, 34–35
    don't try to solve everything all at once, 35–36
empathy, navigating a path to
    find one area of understanding, 38–39
    reflection for, 40–43
    start with the facts, 36–38
excusing, empathizing vs., 39
expectations, setting clear, 21–23

facts, focusing on, 36–38
fear
    mastering, 23–26
    reacting with, 49–50

I don't know, saying, 25–26
impostor syndrome, 3
innovator, the jittery, 9–10. *See also* school reform
instructional feedback, avoiding the pitfalls of
    don't nitpick for lack of real suggestions, 127–128
    don't punt by claiming inexperience, 128–129
instructional feedback, navigating a path to
    ask for feedback on your feedback, 136
    ask reflective questions, 134–136
    demonstrate eagerness to learn, 130–131
    rephrase to communicate confidence, 131*f*
    spend time just watching, 129–132

start with student-based observations, 132–134
instructional imposter, the, 124–127

leadership
    doubts and ability to lead, 5–6
    learning about vs. reality of, 1–2
    mythology surrounding, 5

managing up, 59–63
mindfulness, 3
mob mollifier, the, 86–90
mobs, avoiding the pitfalls of
    don't bargain, 91–92
    don't clap back, 90–91
    don't damage your reputation, 91
    don't feel compelled to answer everything immediately, 92–93
    don't reward unprofessional behavior, 92
mobs, navigating
    break them into small groups, 100
    compel written vs. spoken participation, 99
    increase contributing voices, 99–100
    know when to pull the plug, 101–104
    listen more than you talk, 93–96
    lower the temperature, 100–101
    project eager interest, 95
    recognize you're not going to win, 93–94
    speak to individuals, not the mob, 79–81
    structure the conversation, 96–101
    use nonverbal communication, 100–101
multipliers, 24–25

No Child Left Behind (NCLB) Act, 11

omniscience, 23, 25
others, seeing as intelligent, 24–25

parking lot tactic, 97
perspective, putting change in, 70–73
political credit, building, 61
principals, average tenure length, 11–12
problems, solving, 25, 35–36
promises, making, 70
punching bag, avoiding becoming the boss's
  build political credit, 62
  collect facts, 47
  cover your assets, 61
  document, 61–62
  don't assume your boss is entirely wrong or right, 47–49
  don't react emotionally, 49–50
punching bag, navigate a path to defuse fury
  ask yourself why a reasonable person would act this way, 52–55
  document and share progress, 56
  express as much agreement as you can, 50–52
  manage up, 59–63
  prioritize fixing the problem, 55–59
punching bag, the boss's
  perception as reality, 48, 55–59
  you as the, 44–47

questions
  asking during confrontations, 52–55
  asking the extra, 25
  legitimate vs. frivolous issues, 77, 78*f*
  reflective, 134–136
  thinking strategically to find answers, 76–77
questions, answering
  mob, 92–93, 96–99
  with nonverbal communication, 100–101
  with questions, 94
  refusing to, 92–93
  tone when, 95, 98
  when ready, 73–75
  without thinking, 25–26
questions, unworthy
  answering with questions, 96–97
  disingenuous, 15
  exposing unworthiness, 98
  manipulative, 15
  parking lot tactic, 97
  refusing to answer, 92–93
  relegating, 16
  responding by calling out meritless qualities, 98
  unrealistic, 15

reflection
  for change, 72–73
  emotional intelligence and, 40–43

salesperson, the struggling, 64–68. *See also* selling change
school reform, avoiding resistance to
  don't create a plan in isolation, 13–14
  don't let unworthy questions derail you, 14–16
  don't promise unconditional success, 14
school reform, navigating a path to
  doubts, mitigating, 21–22
  focus on progress, not success, 19–21

school reform, navigating a path to (*cont'd*)
  master your fear, 23–26
  sell the collaboration as much as the plan, 16–19
  set clear expectations, 21–23
school reform, resistance to
  the deadliest pitfall, 14
  by insulting teachers, 13
  reasons for, 11–13
self-doubt
  causes underlying, 3–4
  responding to, 6–7
  sharing, 140–141
  voicing, responses to, 2–3
self-doubt, truths about
  doubts do not hinder your leadership ability, 5–6
  they are inevitable, 139
  you are not alone, 4
  you are not broken, 139
  you are not incompetent, 5
self-image, changing your, 23–26
self-talk, emotionally intelligent, 42
selling change, avoiding the pitfalls when
  don't invent a rationale, 69
  don't make promises you can't keep, 70
  don't say "the district is making us do this," 68–69
  maintain credibility, 68–69
selling change, navigating a path when
  be receptive, not reactive, 73–75
  calibrate and construct answers, 76–79
  decide whether you can embrace the change, 81–84
  enforcing with moral or ethical conflicts, 82–84
  put the change in perspective, 70–73
  speak to individuals, not the mob, 79–81
short straw, the, 106–110
short-straw assignments, avoiding the pitfalls of
  don't phone it in, 112–113
  don't try to get out of it, 110–112
  remember your reputation is your most valuable asset, 111
  ripple effects, remember the, 111–112
  this might be a golden opportunity, 112
short-straw assignments, navigating a path
  control the narrative, 113–116
  document and verify meticulously, 115–116
  investigate pressure points, 117–118
  involve others, 113–115
  leverage your success, 120–122
  turn critics into comrades, 116–119
silent, when to remain, 33–34
speech, monitoring your, 33–34
success, promising unconditional, 14

teacher advocates for change
  celebrating, 20
  crediting, 17
  devoured by colleagues, 17–18
  preparing and supporting, 18

uncertainty, embracing, 25–26

About the Author

Elizabeth Dampf is a practicing administrator in the Chicagoland area, where she has served at both the building and district levels. She is the author of several print articles in *Educational Leadership* and regularly contributes to the ASCD blog. Elizabeth has also spoken on several podcasts, including *Leaning into Leadership* and *Principal Liner Notes*. Her conference presentations include "It's About HOW, Not WHAT: Rethinking Professional Learning Systems in a Time of Scarcity, Tension, and Turnover" (Large Unit District Association, 2023), "Responding to Staff Turnover with Guaranteed PD Systems" (Illinois Association of School Boards Joint Annual Conference, 2023), and "Worthwhile Walk-Throughs" and "Engaging with Mentors to Improve Teacher Effectiveness" (Learning Forward Annual Conference, 2019).

Related Resources: Educational Leadership

At the time of publication, the following resources were available (ASCD stock numbers in parentheses):

The Assistant Principal 50: Critical Questions for Meaningful Leadership and Professional Growth by Baruti K. Kafele (#121018)

The Assistant Principal Identity: Protecting Your Leadership Mindset, Fervor, and Authenticity by Baruti K. Kafele (#123049)

Embracing MESSY Leadership: How the Experience of 20,000 School Leaders Can Transform You and Your School by Alyssa Gallagher and Rosie Connor (#124011)

The EQ Way: How Emotionally Intelligent School Leaders Navigate Turbulent Times by Ignacio Lopez (#123046)

Finding Your Leadership Soul: What Our Students Can Teach Us About Love, Care, and Vulnerability by Carlos R. Moreno (#123025)

Navigating the Principalship: Key Insights for New and Aspiring School Leaders by James P. Spillane and Rebecca Lowenhaupt (#118017)

The Principal Reboot: 8 Ways to Revitalize Your School Leadership by Jen Schwanke (#121005)

Small Shifts, Meaningful Improvement: Collective Leadership Strategies for Schools and Districts by P. Ann Byrd, Alesha Daughtrey, Jonathan Eckert, and Lori Nazareno (#123007)

What If I'm Wrong? And Other Key Questions for Decisive School Leadership by Simon Rodberg (#121009)

What's Your Leadership Story? A School Leader's Guide to Aligning How You Lead with Who You Are by Gretchen Oltman and Vicki Bautista (#121020)

For up-to-date information about ASCD resources, go to www.ascd.org. You can search the complete archives of *Educational Leadership* at www.ascd.org/el. To contact us, send an email to member@ascd.org or call 1-800-933-2723 or 703-578-9600.

iste+ascd

Transform Instruction to
Transform Students' Lives

Our Transformational Learning Principles (TLPs) are evidence-based practices that ensure students have access to high-impact, joyful learning experiences.

Endorsed by AASA and NASSP, the TLPs provide a shared language and a framework for reimagining teaching and learning, focusing on nurturing student growth, guiding intellectual curiosity, and empowering learners to take ownership of their education.

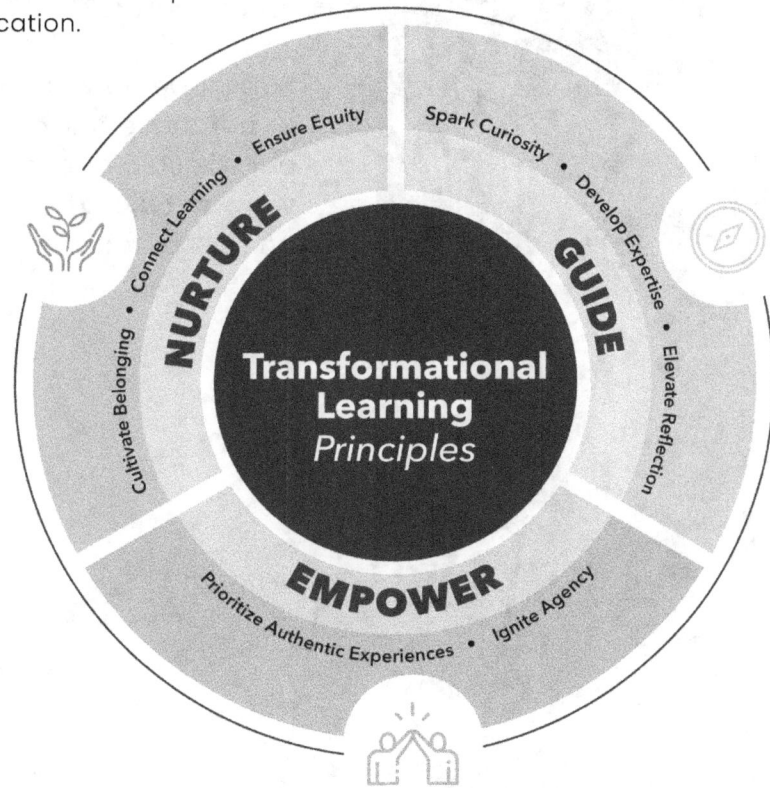

Learn more at **ascd.org/tlps**

DON'T MISS A SINGLE ISSUE OF THIS AWARD-WINNING MAGAZINE.

iste+ascd
educational leadership

If you belong to a Professional Learning Community, you may be looking for a way to get your fellow educators' minds around a complex topic. Why not delve into a relevant theme issue of *Educational Leadership*, the journal written by educators for educators?

Subscribe now and browse or purchase back issues of our flagship publication at **www.ascd.org/el**. Discounts on bulk purchases are available.

iste+ascd

Arlington, VA USA
1-800-933-2723

www.ascd.org
www.iste.org

www.ingramcontent.com/pod-product-compliance
Lightning Source LLC
Chambersburg PA
CBHW070606010526
44118CB00012B/1457